Working with Plastics

Rosario Capotosto

Drawings by
Eugene Thompson

Popular Science Books

Contents

Acknowledgments

The author thanks the following persons for their kind assistance in the preparation of this book: Viola W. Bostic, Lenora Cerrato, William J. Cleary, Jr., Cynthia Cook, George M. Drake, John R. Gill, M. J. Heffernan, Anne L. McIntosh and Howard J. Williams, Jr.

Also thanks to the following firms for supplying data and for permission to use copyrighted material: Dremel Tools, E. I. DuPont Company, Formica Corporation, Gray & Rogers, Inc., McKone & Company, Inc., Rohm & Haas Company, Ralph Wilson Plastics Company.

Sincere thanks also to Henry Gross, editor at Popular Science Books, for his guidance in the planning and production of the book.

1 | Cast Acrylics

Working with acrylics can be a wonderful way to utilize leisure time. The medium is a natural for sparking your imagination to produce numerous decorative and functional articles and furnishings for the home.

The basic skills can be learned in relatively short order, and once you acquire them you will be prepared to tackle practically any job, regardless of its seeming complexity. The more sophisticated project will require more time, but the procedures will essentially be the same as for a simple one. So, if you have a desire to do it yourself with a fascinating material, try your hand with acrylics.

Acrylic plastic is a unique material with several desirable properties. Foremost among them is ease of fabrication.

Acrylic can be sawed, drilled, and machined in much the same manner as hardwood or soft metal with hand or power tools. When heated to a pliable state with relatively moderate temperature the material can be formed into a wide variety of interesting and functional shapes. Strong transparent joints are made quickly by applying a special solvent cement which welds the parts together. Easily polished to a brilliant high luster, the finished product possesses a sparkling clarity equal to that of cut crystal.

An important aspect of working with acrylics: Although a workshop equipped with a variety of power tools is advantageous, it definitely is not essential. A few basic household tools, a clamp-on woodworking vise, several low-cost accessories, and a kitchen table will suffice as a suitably equipped "shop" for a variety of projects if work space and your tool chest are of moderate proportions.

Other favorable properties account for the wide acceptance and popularity of acrylic as a functional and crafting material. It weighs about half as much as glass of comparable thickness and has much greater impact resistance. When subjected to impact beyond its resistance it breaks into large, relatively dull-edged pieces which considerably reduce the hazard

The acrylic cube, a simple construction, has become a decorating classic, and has limitless design possibilities. Here a 16″ cube has been used to protect a piece of sculpture and to support a 12″ terrarium.

Rohm and Haas Company

of injury. This makes it an ideal safety-glazing material for doors, windows, and shower doors. Added to the back of a glass-paned door, a ¼″ thick sheet of this tough material effectively deters intruders. Also, as glazing, acrylic sheet is about 20% better than glass in terms of thermal insulation.

Cell-cast acrylic in colorless form has exceptional transparency equal to that of the finest optical glass. Its total white-light transmittance is 92%. It withstands exposure to weather and sun and has excellent resistance to most household chemicals.

Technically acrylic is a cast thermoplastic material produced from methyl methacrylate resins derived from natural resources. The liquid resins are cast in a mold which renders the final form: plain or patterned sheets as well as rods and tubes. The rigid, resilient material is available colorless and in a variety of colors.

Acrylics are produced by a number of manufacturers and marketed under specific trade names. Among the most common are Plexiglas (Rohm and Haas), Polycast (Polycast Technology), Lucite (DuPont), and Acrylite (American Cyanamid).

AVAILABILITY.   You can obtain acrylic plastic and related accessories from several sources. Until recently, the usual sources of supply were craft-supply stores and plastics distributors. Presently, however, the mate-

A drill, saw, and heat lamp are the basic tools required to make this wine server. Acrylic plastic can be bent with heat.

rial is becoming more widely available at hardware stores, glazing dealers, and home-improvement and building-supply centers. These outlets may stock only a limited number of sizes but they usually will place special orders to meet your requirements.

The best place to shop for the material is at the plastics distributors. Here you will find a vast inventory of sizes, shapes, colors, and patterns. Since most distributors are also engaged in fabrication activities, they usually accumulate a quantity of cut-off pieces which they sell at retail. By scrounging around the odd-size bins and racks you can frequently find pieces to meet your needs, thus minimizing cost. Generally, regardless of where you buy, you pay for cutting and waste when ordering non-stock sizes.

The distributor may also have bundles of random-sized scraps which are sold by the pound at reduced cost—a good way to build up your own stockpile for small projects. If you don't know the location of a distributor in your area, check the Yellow Pages of your phone directory. They are listed under the heading "Plastics—Rods, Tubes, Sheets, Etc.—Supply Centers."

SIZES. Acrylic sheet is available in sizes up to 67″ × 102″ and in thicknesses from .030″ to 4.0″. It is sold by the square foot. The thicknesses

Use thin stock to economize
when structural strength is
not required, as in this
simple hanging shelf.

Rohm and Haas Company

generally utilized for craft and home improvement work are $\frac{1}{10}''$, $\frac{1}{8}''$, $\frac{3}{16}''$, $\frac{1}{4}''$, and $\frac{1}{2}''$. Rods come in diameters from $\frac{1}{16}''$ to 3″ and in lengths up to 6′. They're available polished and unpolished, depending upon the method of manufacture. Cast rod is polished, extruded rod is not. Cast tubes run from $1\frac{1}{2}''$ to 6″ in diameter and up to 6′ in length. Wall thicknesses vary from $\frac{1}{8}''$ to $\frac{1}{2}''$. Additional shapes available include triangles, half-rounds, square rods, balls, and blocks.

COLORS.   Sheets are available in bright transparent, translucent and opaque colors, and translucent white and opaque black as well as gray and bronze transparent tints of varying densities. Transparent colors provide clear "see-through" visibility, while translucent colors transmit light that is diffused so that an object behind the sheet cannot be clearly distinguished. Patterned sheets in transparent colors are also available. Their various surface textures refract transmitted light and provide decorative effects.

TYPES.   Acrylics are produced in several formulations to meet industrial and commercial requirements. Two formulations are generally available at the retail level—standard and glazing grade. For example, in the Rohm and Haas product line, which is widely marketed in the consumer trade, these would be classified as Plexiglas G and Plexiglas MC, respectively. Type G is a general-purpose grade ideally suited for craft work as well as for safety glazing. Type MC is the more economical safety-glazing grade. The important difference between the two is that Plexiglas MC cannot be capillary-cemented with a solvent cement. On the other hand, Plexiglas MC is formulated to give superior thermoformability.

Acrylic sheet is covered on both sides with a pressure-sensitive adhesive-backed kraft paper which can be readily removed by peeling. The masking paper protects the surface of the sheet against accidental scratching during normal handling and fabricating operations. It should be kept intact and in place for most cutting and machining operations. However, it must be removed from both sides for heat forming.

STORAGE.   Masked sheets should never be stored outdoors. Exposure to sunlight for longer than a few days makes the removal of the masking paper extremely difficult.

The best way to store the material is vertically on end, avoiding an angled tilt. A leaning sheet will eventually bow, and this could cause problems if the project at hand requires the use of perfectly flat stock. Small pieces can be stacked on a shelf, provided they are neatly arranged with the larger pieces below, smaller ones above. A helter-skelter pile with pieces overhanging will also cause distortions.

2 | Design Considerations

The use of acrylic plastic as a craft material offers the potential for designing and producing a variety of interesting and useful articles. However, there are several factors to consider during the planning stage of a project, including economy, structural soundness, formability, and the use of mock-up models.

ECONOMY. Acrylic, like practically all other materials nowadays, is relatively expensive, so you should plan carefully to minimize cost. There are several ways to do this. First, avoid overbuilding. For example, a model display case which serves only to protect the contents against dust need not be made with stock greater than ⅛″ in thickness. The same holds true for a tabletop protector or a small curio shelf. When structural strength is not essential, opt for the thinner-gauge material.

Find out what stock sizes are available at your source of supply and try to keep your design within those bounds if feasible. Otherwise you may be required to purchase an additional piece simply to gain an inch or two. Or, if you order a nonstandard size which must be cut from a larger piece, you pay extra for cutting and waste, as stated earlier. More often than not, a slight reduction in project size will not be of great consequence. Odd-shaped sections can be very wasteful of material if a cutting layout is not planned in advance.

Finally, you can use acrylic in combination with a lower-priced material such as ordinary plywood. For example, you can construct the basic form with wood for sturdiness, then apply a thin translucent or opaque acrylic facing to conceal the substrate. Wood sections, painted or stained, may also be exposed to view as integral parts of the design.

STRUCTURAL SOUNDNESS. Strength should be a prime consideration in design. Tables, load-bearing shelves, freestanding or wall-hung cabinets, and the like should be constructed with material at least ¼″

Unitized leg and cross-member design is attractive and strong, but extra care must be exercised in planning the cutting layout to avoid waste.

thick. Legs or other two-sided corner members can be strengthened with gussets. Shelves gain extra strength when longitudinal cleats are added to the underside.

Mechanical fasteners such as screws and bolts make good assemblies provided they are surrounded by sufficient wall thickness when inserted into an edge. A good rule of thumb: Material thickness should be at least twice the diameter of the threaded section of the fastener.

If a router or table saw is available, consider the use of simple woodworking joints such as dadoes and rabbets for added strength. Also, both these tools can be used to cut decorative molded edges in thick stock.

FORMABILITY. Being a thermoplastic material (bendable when heated), acrylic affords a wide range of design possibilities. A primary advantage of this property is that it allows constructions with minimal cemented joints. A formed corner is strong, frequently looks better than a cemented joint, and is easier and quicker to accomplish.

Forming also adds rigidity to flat sheets and should be considered in design as a means to prevent "cold-flow." This is a condition wherein a horizontally installed sheet of acrylic deflects under load or, in sufficient time, under its own weight, resulting in a permanent deformation. Shaping the sheet along the edges effectively avoids the problem.

In designing projects which include continuous straight-line bends, the length of the bend must necessarily be limited to the size of the heating unit. The strip heater (described later), which is ideally suited for home-shop applications, can handle bends up to 34" in length.

Combine acrylic with wood to add interest while minimizing materials cost. This handsome piece is a good example of how the two materials can complement each other.

Rohm and Haas Company

Rohm and Haas Company

This one-piece table is basically a simple project, but the bends must be made in proper sequence.

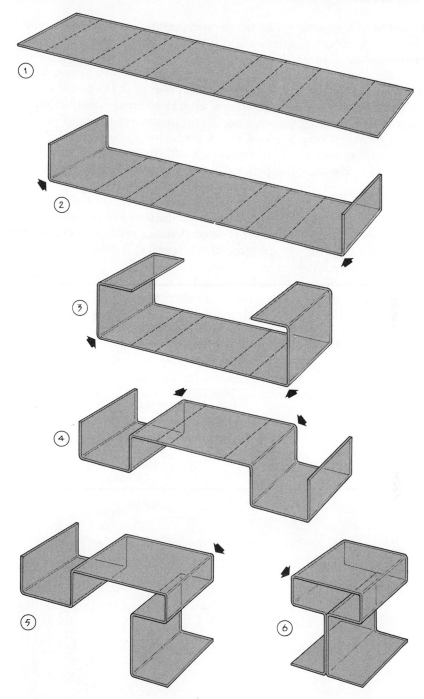

Rohm and Haas Company

This diagram shows the bending sequence for the table. A folded paper model for a project such as this helps to work out any problems in advance. Always indicate the bend lines on the appropriate side of the model (note arrows).

MODELS.   Designing your own projects can be a rewarding experience if the finished product satisfies the intended function and is pleasing in appearance. Sometimes, however, an end result, although made according to plan, just doesn't come across as a success because of some shortcoming in the original concept which was not apparent in the two-dimensional drawing. This is a common problem which can easily be avoided by the simple device of making a scale model or, in some cases, a full-size mock-up. This need not be a work of art. A crude but fairly accurately dimensioned construction made of cardboard or paper will suffice. This will enable you to visualize the project in terms of its three-dimensional reality.

Size relationships, proportions, and overall appearance can be studied in the model to determine whether modifications are in order. Changes in the plans are easily made at this stage. A major change in design during construction or after completion of the project could prove costly in materials, time, and effort.

In some situations a model is essential to prove the feasibility of an unusual design. For projects which include numerous heat-formed bends, a model is needed to aid in determining the "plan of action" for the bending sequence. When working on the actual project a bend in the wrong order can trap you into a corner, so to speak, thus preventing further bends. Usually a model for this purpose can consist merely of a sheet of paper with the fold lines clearly indicated.

3 | Measuring and Marking

When you have decided on what you want to make and have the plans and material on hand, you're ready for the first step: the layout—measuring and marking the working lines on the stock to guide in cutting or shaping to the finished form.

The tools required for layout are relatively few and the techniques for using them quite simple. A typical kit would include: pencil, pen, china marker, aluminum or steel rule, combination square, awl, compass, divider, and possibly several French curves.

The protective masking paper on plain acrylic sheet is an ideal surface on which to draw directly with pencil or pen. Textured panels, rods, tubes, and sometimes blocks come unmasked. A china-marking pencil will adhere nicely on the unmasked materials, but the resultant mark is normally too thick and uneven to provide reasonable accuracy for any exacting work. There are several ways to mark unmasked stock. On textured panels a strip of masking tape is applied in the area to be marked, in approximate position. The line is then drawn on the tape.

The masking-tape method may also be used on other than textured panels, but for greater precision the awl is used. This is a sharp-pointed tool which is sometimes called a scratch awl, and that's exactly what it does; it scratches the surface. The resultant scribed line is distinct and easy to see. It is a definite scratch which cannot be removed; therefore it is important to scribe only on actual cutting lines. Otherwise the scratch will remain in the surface of the finished work. A word of caution: Under no circumstances should a line be scribed in an area where the stock is to be heat-formed, because the scratch would develop into a crack when the plastic is bent. The china marker is used to indicate bend lines.

If the layout on unmasked stock involves a complex design, it is advisable to draw the pattern on paper which can then be rubber-cemented onto the surface. This approach is also recommended on masked stock when the lettered imprint on the masking tends to become confusing with

11

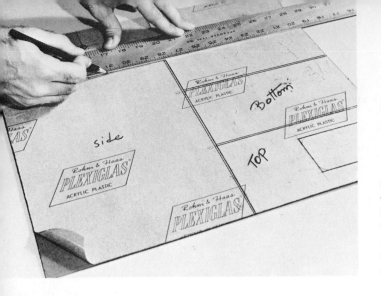

Sawblades have thickness, which wastes some material in the form of sawdust. When precision is important the layout should be drawn with double lines to allow for the waste.

small patterns. Ordinary art rubber cement is the kind to use. For best results it should be of fairly thin consistency and applied to both surfaces.

Some projects won't require precision marking to any significant degree while others will, particularly when a number of pieces must be joined together to make up the final assembly. Assuming the latter, it is important to check the initial working edge of masked stock before making the first measurement or mark. Frequently masking paper overhangs the "factory" edge slightly. This will prevent the rule or square from making positive contact with the true edge of the stock. A sawed edge should also be checked in advance because it may exhibit small lumps of paper and gummed adhesive. Overhanging paper can be trimmed flush to the edge with a razor blade. Lumps are removed by lightly sanding with fine abrasive paper wrapped around a block of wood.

KERF ALLOWANCE. There are two methods of cutting stock—by scribing and breaking, and by sawing. The procedures are discussed in the next chapter, but the way you lay out the cutting lines must take into account the method of cutting which is anticipated. Cuts made by scribing will result in no waste. Saw cuts do result in waste in an amount equal to the thickness of the blade. Therefore, the kerf (the slit or space) made by the blade must be considered and allowance made accordingly for work that is being marked for sawing. For example, three pieces 3″ wide can be obtained from a piece of stock 9″ wide if the cuts are made by scribing. On the other hand, assuming the use of a sawblade ⅛″ thick, the stock would have to be 9¼″ wide to permit sawing the three 3″ pieces.

This illustrates the necessity of indicating the kerf waste factor when marking stock for sawing a number of parts from a single sheet of material. The best way to do this is by drawing double lines. If available, a felt-tip pen which makes a line equal to the thickness of the sawblade could prove to be a timesaver.

TUBES AND RODS.   Marking tubes and rods for cutting or drilling requires some special but simple techniques, as follows:

• To scribe a line along the length of a tube, lay it on its side, then press a piece of wood up against it and draw an awl along the top edge of the guide.

• To scribe a line around the circumference of a tube, a V-shaped trough with a stop at one end is used. Hold the point of the awl at the desired location, then slowly revolve the tube while pressing it lightly against the end stop.

• To make accurately spaced marks on the circumference, cut a strip of paper to length so it fits around the tube with the ends just meeting. Remove the paper from the tube, lay it out flat, and divide it into the required number of marks. Tape the paper into place on the tube, then transfer the marks with the awl.

GEOMETRIC SHAPES.   Irregular curves and geometric shapes are sometimes required for projects. Smooth-flowing graceful curves are usually more interesting than ordinary circles or arcs, and they are quite easy to develop. The best way for small patterns is with the use of French curves. These are transparent plastic templates which are available at art-supply stores in a wide variety of shapes. Various curves are made by drawing directly against the edges.

For large freeform curves a strip of flexible material such as wood, plastic, or metal can be bent into the desired shape and held in place while a line is drawn against the edge.

Hexagons and octagons.   These are often used in layouts for tabletops and other projects. The hexagon has six equal sides and the octagon eight equal sides.

To draw a hexagon, set a compass to draw a circle with a radius equal to one side of the shape. Set the point of the compass at any location on the circle and strike an arc on the circle. Move the compass point to the

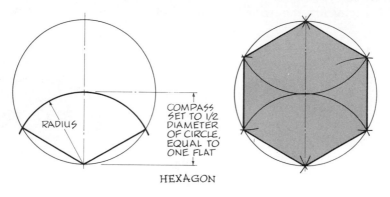

HEXAGON

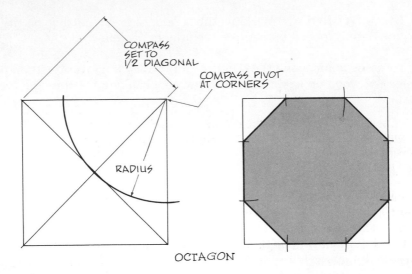

OCTAGON

intersection of the arc and strike another arc, and so on, until six arcs are made on the circumference. Then connect the points with a straightedge.

For an octagon, draw a square equal to the overall size of the octagon. Draw diagonal lines to cross each corner, then set the compass to one-half the length of the diagonal. Using the corners of the square as centers, strike arcs to intersect the sides of the square. Connect the points where the arcs intersect the sides of the square.

Ellipses.   Another popular form is the flattened circle or ellipse. There are several ways to draw an ellipse, but the following method is probably the simplest.

Draw two lines equal to the major and minor axes at right angles to each other to form a cross. Adjust the compass to half the longer axis. Set the point at one end of the shorter line and strike an arc to intersect two points on the longer line. Drive a nail at each of these points—the compass center point and each of the arc intersections. Tie a string around the three nails, then replace the center-point nail with a pencil. Hold the pencil straight and bear it against the string to draw the ellipse. Note: Drill pilot holes for

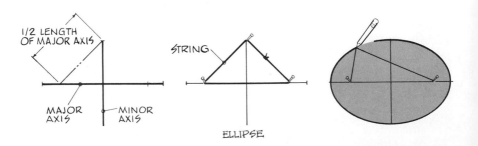

ELLIPSE

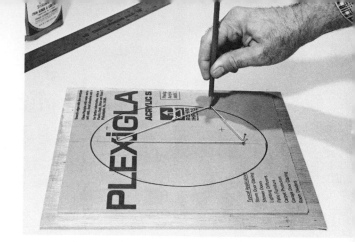

The string used for drawing an ellipse must be nonelastic. Keep pencil perpendicular.

the nails. If the center of the ellipse is to be used, draw the shape on paper, then transfer the outline to the work.

ENLARGING WITH SQUARES. Project plans found in books and magazines frequently are drawn in reduced size to fit the page. If the plan contains irregular contours it usually will be drawn against a grid of small squares with a notation of the size of the full-scale squares to be drawn to enlarge the pattern. For example, each square may represent 1″. This is called enlarging with squares, and the procedure is quite simple: On a large sheet of paper draw 1″ squares to equal the number of squares in the small drawing. Number the vertical and horizontal squares to correspond with the squares in the drawing. Working one square at a time, lightly draw a line through the large square in the same position that it is located in the corresponding small square. Continue adding the lines until the full pattern is drawn. French curves can be used to smooth and darken the lines. The pattern can be traced onto the work with carbon paper, or it can be cut out and used as a template.

Enlarging with squares.

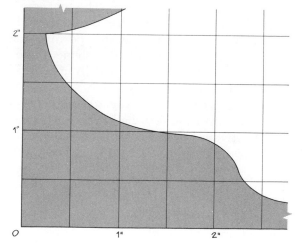

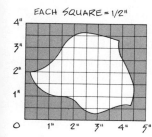

4 | Cutting Acrylics

Acrylic plastic can be cut in two ways—by scribing and breaking, and by sawing. An acrylic scriber is used for the first method. For sawing, a wide variety of hand and power saws can be used. The choice among the hand tools includes the coping saw, hacksaw, backsaw, keyhole saw, and regular hand saw. For power sawing you can use the portable saber saw and circular saw or the stationary jigsaw, band saw, and table saw.

Although the techniques of working with the various power saws are discussed in the pages that follow, bear in mind that while power tools are definitely advantageous, they are not absolutely essential for working with acrylics. Actually, many projects can be fabricated without any saw at all.

SCRIBING AND BREAKING. Sheet material can be effectively cut to size by scribing the surface and breaking, somewhat in the manner that glass is cut. This method is used for making straight cuts in stock up to ¼" thick. A low-cost scriber is available where acrylics are sold and at many hardware stores as well. The tool consists of a hardened steel blade which cuts as it is drawn backward with the handle held in an almost horizontal position. This affords positive control and maximum cutting action with minimal effort. The shape of the blade permits resharpening or touching up to a keen point by merely filing or honing a flat on the surface of the leading edge.

A straightedge is used to guide the tool to make an accurate cut. This can be a metal rule or a shallow strip of hardwood which has a true edge. For relatively small cuts up to about 18" in length, the guide may be hand-held, but for longer runs it should be clamped in place.

Thicknesses from ¹⁄₁₀" to ³⁄₁₆" will require five or six passes of the tool to scribe deeply enough for a clean break. Stock ¼" thick will require seven to ten passes.

Scribing must be done with the material supported on a flat, sturdy work surface. The point is placed at the far edge of the sheet and drawn firmly

A clamped straightedge guide is necessary to scribe long workpieces with accuracy.

against the guide until it runs off the near edge. After scribing, the sheet is broken apart, as follows.

The scribed line, face up, is positioned over a ¾"-diameter wood dowel as long as or longer than the workpiece. Starting near an end, downward pressure is applied with the palms of the hands to both sides of the line. As the break progresses the hands are accordingly repositioned, keeping them adjacent to each other.

This method is normally used only for making continuous cuts from edge to edge, but there is a trick worth knowing: Assume you want to cut out a rectangular section 4" × 48" from a larger piece of stock. The usual procedure would be to make two saw cuts. However, you can save a lot of time by combining a saw and scribe cut. Make the 4" cut first, using the saw. Then scribe and break the 48" portion to meet the first cut.

The scribing method is not workable for cutoffs under 1½" or for patterned sheet. For these the saw is needed.

Left: Apply firm pressure and draw the cutting point of the scribing tool across the full length of the material. The guide can be hand-held for short cuts. *Right.* The scribed line is positioned face up over a wood dowel running the length of the intended break. Apply downward pressure with both hands.

Rohm and Haas Company.

HAND SAWING. A crosscut hand saw with 14 or more teeth per inch will perform best among all the hand saws for cutting long sheet material. Clamp the sheet to the work table with a stiff board above and close to the cutting line. Steadied this way the piece won't chatter, thus permitting an accurate cut. The saw should be slanted back at an angle of about 45° for best results. Note that a crosscut saw is specified—a ripsaw should be avoided because its deeply set teeth will cause excessive chipping along the cut edge.

A smoother cut with greater accuracy can be obtained with a backsaw, which has finer teeth and a stiffer blade than the hand saw. However, due to its thick spine (back), this saw cannot be used to make cuts of long dimension; the back gets in the way. Its use is limited to cuts in stock of about 6" in width. It is particularly suited for cutting accurate miters and right angles on small pieces, including rods and tubes. For flat stock this saw is not held like the hand saw; it is not slanted but the teeth ride flat on the surface of the work.

The hacksaw is also useful for making crosscuts on small workpieces. The metal-cutting blade cuts rather smoothly and will stay sharp longer than the wood-cutting saws. Like the backsaw, the hacksaw frame prevents long cuts except along an edge. A long continuous cut can be made parallel to the edge by rotating the frame to the side. The width of the cut is limited, however, to the throat capacity, which is usually about 4".

Curved and irregular cuts are made with the coping saw. This saw is used with the blade held in the vertical position, handle at the bottom and teeth pointing downward. The work should be supported on both sides of the cut. This is best accomplished by clamping a board with a V-notch cut into the end, overhanging the work table. Internal cuts which do not open to an outside edge are made by drilling a small hole for blade entry in the waste area. The blade is inserted through the hole, then attached to the frame. This saw, too, has throat size limitations which vary from 6" to 12".

The keyhole saw has a narrow blade and can be used for cutting large-radius curves but it is particularly useful for making internal cuts without workpiece size limitations.

As a general rule, in most fabrications of appreciable size where the shape of the work involves an inside corner, it is advisable to avoid sharp corners. Instead, an inside corner should have a small radius. This can be accomplished by predrilling a small hole at the corner before sawing. The curvature reduces the possibility of future fracture due to stress concentrations.

POWER SAWING. Whatever the hand saws can do, the power saws will do faster. The choice of equipment will depend on what you have available and the type of work to be done. Portable and table circular saws are used to make straight cuts. The band saw is good for large-curve cutting and also for straight work, though its straight cuts are less precise than the circular saw's. The jigsaw is used for the fancy cuts, and it too does reasonably well on straight cuts with the proper blade. The saber saw is a good all-around tool for straight and intricate work. If you had to make a choice of using only one power tool, the versatile saber saw should perhaps be the one.

Some general rules to observe when working acrylics with power saws:

• Use only sharp blades. Dull blades cause friction and heat.

• Feed the work (or saw) slowly. Forced feeding also produces heat. This could cause the material to soften sufficiently at the kerf to result in resealing of the cut with melted and rehardened chips and sawdust.

• Keep machines and materials clean. Acrylic particles are electrostatic and tend to cling to the work and machine surfaces. A buildup could cause scratches and definitely will prevent proper close contact between the work and machine surfaces.

• Use the proper blade. Only sharp blades with at least 6 teeth per inch, and all the same height and point-to-point distance, should be used. Those with large gullets and excessive set should be avoided. The former will clog and the latter will cause chipping.

• Cut only masked material. The masking paper helps clear the cut, avoiding gumming behind the blade. Apply strips of masking tape to both sides of the intended cut before sawing unmasked material.

SABER SAW.   The sawing operation for most projects can be accomplished with the saber saw. It cuts on the upstroke; therefore it is important to work on a sturdy surface so that ample pressure can be exerted to hold the work down to overcome the tendency of the work and saw to vibrate and bounce upward. Use a metal-cutting blade or special blades which are designed for cutting acrylics. For acrylic thicknesses of 1/8" and less the blade should have at least 24 teeth per inch, and for thicknesses of 3/16" and greater it should have 18 teeth per inch.

The saw is used freehand for cutting irregular shapes, but precise straight-line cuts necessitate the use of a clamped straightedge guide. Whenever possible, clamp the work between the workbench and guide. If the guide must be clamped to the work only, be sure to use scrap blocks below so the clamps are not in direct contact with the plastic. The guide should overhang the work at least 6" at each end to allow the saw to be guided straight as it enters and leaves the work.

Internal cutouts.   To make an internal cut to drop out a square, rectangle, or a shape other than a circle, a hole equal in diameter to the thickness of the material is drilled at each corner. Such blade-entry holes should be

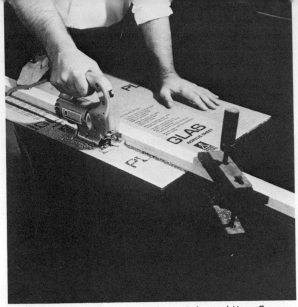

Precise straight cuts can be made with a saber saw by guiding the tool with a straightedge. Do not force-feed.

Rohm and Haas Company

large enough to allow the blade to be positioned tangent to the cutting line if the straight portion is to blend smoothly into the radius. The straight-edge is positioned to guide the saw from hole to hole.

Circular cuts. An accessory pivot guide is used to make circular cuts with the saber saw. If the work will not be disturbed by the presence of a small hole at the center, this method will produce very good results. However, a pivot-guided saw will track in a true circle only if the pivot point and the front edge of the blade are in perfect alignment. This can be checked out by measuring the distances between the front edge of the blade teeth and the pivot point in relation to the guide bar; they must be equal.

The use of blades of varying width can affect the relationship. If there is a discrepancy the cut will spiral in or out, depending upon whether the blade is ahead or behind. In either case, the ends of the cut will not meet. If the guide has a movable pivot it can be adjusted for the blade in use. Otherwise the selection of a blade of the proper width will be necessary. When large pieces of material are involved it is advisable to make a test cut in a piece of scrap wood or cardboard to check the tracking.

To cut a circle, adjust the guide bar for the desired radius, then drill a small pilot hole in the work. Place the pivot in the hole and make the cut. When it is desired to start a cut on the inside of a sheet, a blade-entry hole will be necessary. If more than one circle is contemplated for a given setup, the circle of the largest diameter must be cut first in order to preserve the pivot hole for the following cut(s). An example would be the cutting of a doughnut-shaped ring.

Portable circular saw. This saw is generally associated with rough carpentry work but when equipped with a fine-tooth blade it serves nicely for working with plastics. It is especially useful for making straight, miter,

A portable circular saw equipped with a special acrylic cutting blade does a fast job on big work. It produces a smooth edge.

and bevel cuts on large sheets which are too awkward to handle on the typical home-shop table saw.

A plywood blade is suitable for occasional work, but a special acrylic-cutting blade is available and might be considered if the volume of work warrants the investment. As with the saber saw, a clamped guide is used for making exacting straight cuts. The best way to support the work is by placing it over several lengths of 2 × 3 lumber resting on sawhorses or the workbench.

Plunge cut. A project such as the Parsons table illustrated in Chapter 2 is an ideal candidate for a plunge cut. The one-piece leg and apron sections require an internal cut from leg to leg.

Making a plunge cut with the portable saw necessitates retracting the blade guard, and therefore extra care must be exercised to avoid injury. Tape the guard up and out of the way. A high saw guide such as a piece of 2×4 on edge is clamped to the work. The base of the saw is positioned against the guide with the back of the saw base elevated so the blade is not in contact with the work. The saw is switched on and slowly lowered into the workpiece until the base is resting firmly. The saw is then advanced to continue the cut. The blade must come to a full stop before the saw is removed.

Since the curvature of the blade forms a radial kerf at the beginning and end of an incompleted cut, when working to a corner the underside of the sheet will still be joined by a small web. The cut is completed to the corner with a hand or saber saw.

Jigsaw. With care the jigsaw can be used to cut intricate patterns and curves with small radii in stock up to ½" thickness.

Since the blade has a short stroke of about 1", the constant friction in the small area of the blade which is engaged in cutting produces much

21

heat. The thin, narrow blade contains relatively little metal to dissipate the heat buildup. An overheated blade can melt and mar the plastic along the kerf, resulting in a very poor edge.

Several things can be done to overcome the problem. Run the saw at low speed, feed the work slowly, and frequently lubricate the blade with wax or soap. The choice of the proper blade with respect to the thickness of the material being cut is also very important. As a general rule, the best results are obtained with the following combinations:

Thickness of material	Blade teeth per inch
1/8″	20
1/4″	16
3/8″	12
1/2″	7

Cutting curves.   Cutting curves or irregular shapes with the jigsaw is a relatively simple operation. Before you begin cutting on a complicated pattern, study it to determine the best route to follow. The aim is to eliminate the need to back out of long cuts or to make sharp turns beyond the ability of the blade. Often it will be advantageous to make a detour past small details which can then be approached with separate cuts.

Straight cuts.   In order to do straight cutting with good results, the widest blade possible should be used. A wide blade promotes better heat dissipation and is less apt to twist and wander than a narrow blade.

A board clamped to the tabletop will serve as a fence for cutting strips to exact widths. The fence is also used for cutting bevels when the table is tilted to the required angle. The fence must always be located on the low side of the table when cutting bevels to prevent the work from creeping away from the blade.

Band saw.   The band saw is especially well suited for cutting acrylic in sheet and tubular form. While it is designed primarily for cutting curved or irregular outlines, it performs well on straight work.

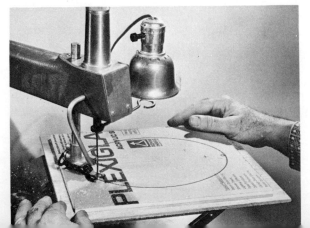

The jigsaw is the tool to use for precision in cutting irregular shapes. A blade-entry hole in the waste area permits you to make internal cuts.

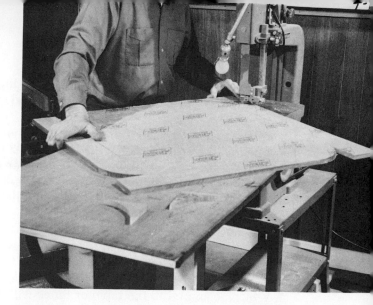

A band-saw blade with 10 teeth per inch cuts through ½" stock with ease. An auxiliary table should be used to support big work.

This saw is closely related to the jigsaw and since the main purpose of both is to make curved cuts, there is an overlap of function. But there are differences which justify the use of one over the other.

On the negative side, the band saw cannot be used to make the intricate cuts which are possible with the jigsaw. Nor can it be used to make internal cuts, because the endless looped blade cannot be threaded into a hole in the workpiece. However, the band saw does have the advantage of speed and the ability to cut thick stock. Also, because of the long length of the blade, heat is quickly dissipated and the problem of a heat-fused kerf is a rare occurrence.

Wood-cutting blades are normally used with good results. Metal-cutting blades can be used, but they have relatively fine teeth and thus are not recommended for cutting stock over ¼" thick.

Cutting stock. Steer the work so the blade cuts a bit away from the outside of the mark to allow sufficient stock for later smoothing. An edge cut with a band saw will have a distinctive corrugated pattern caused by the set of the blade teeth. This is called "washboarding" (because the ripples resemble an old-fashioned washboard).

As with jigsaw work, the path of the cut should be considered in advance to avoid difficulty. Feeding from the wrong direction can get the work into a bind against the saw's column. Sometimes this can't be avoided, in which case it may be necessary to draw the pattern, or part of it, on the underside of the work in order to facilitate completion of the cut from a different starting point.

When cutting a circle it is advisable to lay out the cutting line entirely within the stock rather than to locate it where it borders on an edge. The reason is that a continuous cut will result in greater accuracy. Starting a circular cut at a flat edge without a lead-in is bound to be erratic, and the run-off at the end of the cut will also not be smooth-flowing.

When a number of duplicate parts are needed for a project they can be

23

gang-sawed to save time and, more important, each piece will be exactly alike. A few dabs of rubber cement can be used to join the parts if masking tape cannot be used.

The miter gauge is used to make square or angled cuts. When cutting sharp angles the stock will have a tendency to creep. The problem is solved by taping a piece of fine abrasive paper to the face of the miter gauge, grit side out. Tubing and rods are also cut to length guided by the miter gauge, but they must be fed slowly and held very firmly to prevent them from rotating during the cut.

A rip fence is used to make long straight cuts. If the saw is not equipped with a standard fence, a clamped strip of wood will serve the purpose. The fence can be mounted to the right or left of the blade except when making bevel cuts. Then it must be mounted on the left or down side.

A V block clamped to the table or fence will permit safe and accurate lengthwise cuts in round stock.

Table saw.   The table saw is the precision tool for straight cutting. It is invaluable for cutting acrylics for projects involving cemented joints, which must be perfectly fitted.

All the cuts made with this saw are guided with either the rip fence or miter gauge. The precision is built into the mechanics of the saw; therefore accuracy in measurement and in setting up the guides is about the extent of the skill required to turn out good work.

Several kinds of blades can be used for acrylics. In general, the thicker the material to be cut, the fewer the teeth needed. Accordingly, blades with 6 to 10 teeth per inch are used for thin stock and 3 to 5 teeth for thick material. Crosscut, plywood, or special acrylic-cutting blades work best. The latter two will make the smoothest cuts, while the crosscut is better suited for thick material. These blades are characterized by evenly spaced teeth of the same size and minimal set—factors which reduce or completely avoid chipping. Rip blades have deeply set teeth which cause severe chipping and therefore should be avoided for cutting acrylics.

In all cutting operations the blade should project only slightly above the surface of the stock, about ⅛" to ¼", to obtain the smoothest cut. It may help to lubricate the blade by cutting slightly into a bar of soap. If overheating occurs, the blade must be raised to a greater projection. This reduces heat buildup but generally will result in some chipping. The feed rate should be slowed as the work exits the blade in order to avoid chipping the corners. This holds true with any power or hand saw.

Ripping and crosscutting.   When ripping stock to width, cutting lines rarely need to be marked on the work, since the fence adjustment establishes the dimension. However, it is sometimes advisable to mark the work in order to identify pieces of varying sizes.

If the stock to be cut is large, provision should be made to support the piece as it exits the saw table so it doesn't sag or fall to the floor.

Ripping acrylic plastic on the table saw. Blade cuts smoothest when it projects just slightly above surface. Greater projection like this cuts a bit rougher but cooler.

Normally the working stock is placed between the fence and blade with the waste to the free side of the blade. When very small strips are required, the procedure is reversed because small pieces could become fouled between the blade and fence.

Parts which are to be crosscut are guided with the miter gauge. Unlike working with the rip fence, here the cutoff mark must be made on the work. A scribed line on the edge will afford the best visibility. When making the cut, hold only the gauge-supported piece; never hold the free end or binding will result.

Beveling. Making a bevel rip cut merely requires tilting the blade to the required angle. However, adjustment of the fence requires a different approach than that which is used for a square cut. The reason is that the tilted blade provides no positive reference for measuring to the fence. The following procedure will assure precise results.

The angled cutoff line is marked on the edge of the stock with a scriber and the blade is tilted to the same angle. The fence is set at an arbitrary distance from the blade and a cut is started in a piece of wood scrap.

The piece is backed away from the blade and two marks are made on the table insert to coincide with the kerf in the scrap. This indicates exactly where the cut will occur. The fence is adjusted to align the mark on the work edge to the mark on the table.

Mitering. Mitered cuts are made by adjusting the miter gauge to any angle other than zero. When cutting a miter in acrylic the sharp point of the angle should lead into the blade. This is important. If the point trails it very likely will chip off as the work exits the blade. If such a lead-in approach is not feasible a piece of scrap wood placed between the acrylic and the gauge face will prevent chipping.

Pocket cuts. The pocket or internal cut is used to saw square or rectangular openings in a sheet of plastic. The procedure is quite simple and results in perfectly parallel sections.

The cutting layout must be clearly marked on the surface of the workpiece, and if the inside corners are to be rounded, holes of the appropriate radius should be bored in advance.

If corner holes have been made in the piece, the rip fence is adjusted so that the kerf will be tangent to the holes. This is done by measuring from the edge of the stock to the nearest edge of the hole (to the fence). Set the fence.

Since the initial stage of this cut is done blind, it is advisable to put two marks on the fence which will show the front and back limit of the blade's cutting diameter.

To make the cut, lower the blade so it is below the surface of the table. Place the work in position against the fence, carefully observing the rear limit on the fence. The rear boundary of the cut should be positioned about 2″ beyond the rear mark on the fence. Turn on the power and then, while holding the work down firmly with one hand, crank the blade up until it cuts through the top surface of the stock. Now, using both hands, advance the work until the cut nears the front boundary of the cut. Stop the saw, lower the blade, then reposition the work to make the other cuts.

Note that since the blade cuts a circular-shaped kerf, the partial cut will be longer on the bottom surface than on the top. This is the reason for starting and stopping short of the mark.

If corner holes are present and are of sufficient radius, the cut can be made clear through, from hole to hole. But when corner holes are small or if it is desired to have square corners, the small uncut sections at the corners are finished off with a hand or saber saw to drop out the waste. Inside sharp corners are not recommended on acrylic.

Grooving.   Shallow grooves cut into the surface of clear acrylic sheet will produce an interesting decorative effect.

The rip fence is used to guide the sheet over the blade for this operation. Square-cornered grooves are formed when the blade is used in the normal position. Angled V-grooves can be cut by tilting the blade to 45°. A block of wood is pressed lightly over the sheet at the location of the blade to obtain even contact throughout the cut.

Router.   The router can be used to cut grooves, rabbets, and dadoes and to produce shaped edges on acrylic sheet.

This tool operates at very high speed, usually in excess of 20,000 rpm. Thus a typical bit with two flutes (cutting edges) delivers about 40,000 blade passes on the work per minute. The figure increases to 60,000 with a three-flute bit. This produces heat, a factor which must be considered in the choice of bits.

Router bits are available with and without carbide-tipped flutes and with standard and ball-bearing pilot tips. Due to the relative toughness of acrylic, normal heat buildup would soon remove the temper and dull ordinary bits, resulting in poor work. Therefore only carbide bits should be used.

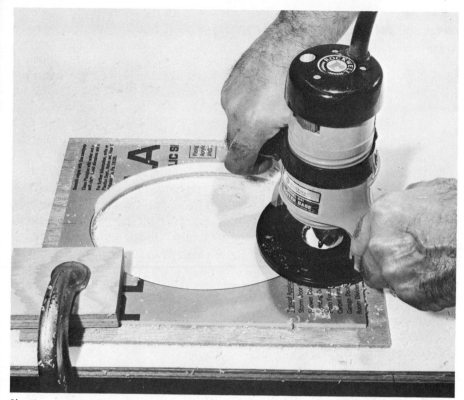

Shaping a cove edge with a router. A plywood scrap is rubber-cemented to the ¼″ acrylic to provide an edge to guide the pilot.

The pilot end rides against the edge of work to control the width of the cut. A standard fixed pilot revolving at considerable speed against the work edge also becomes very hot from friction, resulting in damaging burn marks on the edge. The choice here should be for ball-bearing piloted bits.

The router is used freehand to shape edges with a piloted bit. Non-pilot bits are used to make flat surface cuts such as grooves and dadoes. Some surface cuts can be done freehand, but controlled cuts must be guided with a straightedge or appropriately shaped template clamped to the work.

A trammel point is a useful accessory which guides the router to swing a perfect circle, usually up to 30″ in diameter. With the appropriate bit it can be used to cut circular grooves, shape circular edges, and make circular cutouts.

To shape the edges of small pieces the router is mounted upside down in a vise or a special accessory table which in effect converts the tool into a small stationary shaper. Small pieces can then be pushed across the bit to make the cut.

5 | Making Holes

Plastic projects frequently require holes to serve functional purposes or as elements of the overall design. In either case, true, clean holes are essential for structural soundness and good appearance. A hole made in clear acrylic catches light, which makes it quite conspicious, so its surface should be as smooth as possible. Chipped edges must be avoided not only for appearance but to prevent the possibility of crack formation, which can develop at ragged edges.

TOOLS. Making good holes requires no special skill; it is simply a matter of using the proper tools and procedures.

Standard twist drills used for metals are satisfactory for small holes up to about ³⁄₁₆″. For larger holes high-speed steel drills especially designed for plastics are preferable. Lacking the latter, standard twist drills can be modified to perform satisfactorily.

In general, a drill for acrylics should have cutting lips with zero rake, polished flutes, and an included tip angle of 60°. For very deep holes a point angle up to 140° will perform better. Recommended rpm varies according to drill size—3,000 rpm for drills up to ⅛″, 2,000 for ¼″, and 1,000 and under for ½″ and larger.

To perform properly, drill bits should scrape rather than cut. That's the reason for zero rake—the cutting lip has a blunt rather than a sharp edge. You can readily determine whether the lip rake of your present drill bits need to be modified by making a few test holes in scrap material. If the drill "digs in" and binds, and if the plastic climbs up the drill after the hole breaks through, it is a clear indication that the cutting lips are too sharp. A slight grinding on a wheel or by hand with a stone to flatten the cutting edge will solve the problem.

Drill bits used for metal sometimes have nicks or burrs which will mar the surface of the hole. It's a good idea to set aside some drills for use exclusively on acrylics.

60° ANGLE POINT
FOR THIN STOCK

140° ANGLE POINT
FOR DEEP HOLES

LIP GROUND HERE
FOR ZERO RAKE

Drill-bit points which perform most effectively for acrylics.

You can use a hand drill for holes up to ¼" diameter, but a portable electric drill will be necessary for larger holes. A drill press is a wonderful luxury for any size hole up to 8" diameter. The price of twist drills rises rapidly as the size increases, and home workshops are rarely equipped with bits over ½". But this is of little consequence, because flat wood-boring "spade" bits can be used for holes up to 1¼". They are quite inexpensive and work very well in acrylics due to their scraping action. They cannot be used with hand drills, however; they must be power-driven. For holes between ¾" and 2½" a hole saw will serve the purpose. To cut really large holes up to 8" in diameter, a fly cutter is the proper tool. The hole saw can be used either in a portable drill or in the drill press, but the fly cutter is used only in the press.

When using a hand drill, use a sharp bit, very slow speed, and minimum pressure. Specially ground bits are best with power equipment. Slow the feed as the drill point penetrates the second surface. Wood backup should always be used to avoid chipping.

Rohm and Haas Company

 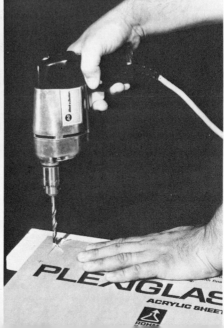

BORING TECHNIQUE

Small Holes. Mark and center-punch the location. The dimple will prevent the drill from skidding about. If the drill is a large one with a web which is larger than the dimple, it may not center properly, in which case the hole should be started with a smaller drill. The small hole, with a diameter equal to or slightly larger than the web of the larger drill, will guide the latter accurately to center.

In any through-drilling operation it is important to back up the work with wood and to reduce the feed pressure as the drill breaks through the underside. Otherwise chipping will occur. Thin stock is especially vulnerable to chipping, but the problem can be avoided by sandwiching it between two pieces of wood with clamps and drilling through the stack.

Deep holes. When drilling other than shallow holes, withdraw the drill occasionally to expel the shavings. Clogged shavings will cause friction and overheating, resulting in roughness of the hole wall. Polished flutes aid in expelling the shavings. Normally, lubrication is not required but is recommended to obtain a more transparent wall in deep holes. Soapy water serves well as a lubricant, but merely brushing it onto the drill or dropping it into the started hole won't do much good because the spiraling motion of the twist drill quickly pumps it out. To obtain good lubrication, first drill a small hole partway through the stock. Fill it with lubricant, then redrill with a bit of the final diameter. If the hole is to go completely through, the pilot hole should be drilled to within about ⅛" of the bottom surface.

A wide drill tip angle, up to 140°, recommended for deep holes, results in a shorter cutting edge and consequently narrower shavings which won't tend to jam up.

Medium-sized holes. A spade bit (or speed bit as it is sometimes called) operated at moderate speed will bore a very smooth-walled hole provided it runs true. Due to its long slender shaft, this bit is prone to bending when not very carefully handled. A bit with even the slightest bend will wobble, resulting in an out-of-round rough cut. When boring deep holes with this bit, occasionally back off slightly—not to eject shavings, which normally do not jam up, but to allow the bit to cool so it doesn't lose its temper.

Hole saws can be used only for through holes, because the waste remains intact until the cut breaks through on the underside of the material. To function properly, hole-saw teeth must have ample set in order to allow clearance for the sawdust which would otherwise be captive in the enclosed kerf. Thus, holes made with this tool usually will not be quite as smooth as those made with drills.

The market is flooded with hole-saw sets sold at bargain prices. They generally should be avoided at any cost, because they usually consist of stamped-out blades which have absolutely no set. In use they literally burn their way into the material, becoming jammed soon after entering the surface.

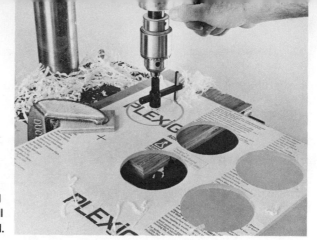

The fly cutter is ideal for making large holes. This tool should be used only in a drill press, never in a portable drill.

Large holes. The fly cutter cuts a clean hole, but you must handle this tool with care because of its excessive thrust. Never use it with a portable drill; it is designed for use only on a drill press. The workpiece should be firmly clamped to the press table. A slow rpm, about 600, is fast enough for this tool. Like the hole saw, it can be used only for making through holes.

CUTTING THREADS.   Some projects which combine acrylic with itself or with other materials such as wood or metal require the cutting of threads in order to facilitate assembly with machine screws.

It is possible to cut satisfactory threads in acrylics using NC (National Course) threading forms. Fine threads should be avoided because of the ease with which the apex fractures.

You must consider wall thickness of the material when selecting a screw which is to be used. If the screw is to enter the edge of the acrylic, its diameter must not be greater than half the thickness of the material. For example, the maximum diameter of a screw which is to be inserted into ½″ stock would be ¼″. If the screw is to enter the face of the stock close to an edge, the same wall allowance applies.

In order to tap good threads, you must first drill a hole of proper size. If the hole is too small, too much material will have to be removed by the tap. This results in rough threads and possible tap breakage. When the

Tapping holes for screws. Refer to the table on page 32 to match drill and tap size. Back off after each full turn to break the chips.

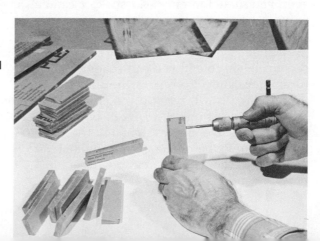

drilled hole is too large the thread will be only partly cut. This will considerably reduce the holding power of the screw. The table below lists the correct tap and drill combinations.

Tap Drill Sizes		
Tap size		Drill Size
Diameter	Threads per inch	Number
4	40	43
6	32	36
8	32	29
10	24	25
12	24	16
¼	20	7
5/16	18	F
3/8	16	5/16
½	13	27/64

The first column indicates the size of the screw in gauge size and in fractions of an inch for the larger screws. The second column refers to the number of threads per inch of the screw. The last column lists the drill size to be used. For example, to drill a hole for a ¼–20 screw a No. 7 drill is required.

There are three kinds of taps: taper, plug, and bottom. The taper tap is smaller at the end to permit easy starting. It must penetrate the work completely to cut a full thread. The plug tap has a slight taper and is used to thread blind holes. The bottom tap has no taper and will cut threads fully to the bottom of a blind hole. To do so, it must be preceded first by the taper, then the plug tap.

Lubricants are not normally necessary for cutting threads, but soapy water will ease the operation. To produce finely finished threads, however, you should insert a wax stick or candle shavings in the hole before tapping.

To tap threads, insert the tapered end of the tap into the drilled hole, press slightly downward, and turn the tap wrench clockwise. Once the threads begin to cut, you can relieve the downward pressure. Continue turning, backing off a quarter-turn after each full turn to break the chips. Sloppy threads will result if the chips are not continually broken.

The outside of round stock can be threaded with a threading die. The dies are available in sizes to match the various tap sizes. The stock to be threaded must be of the correct diameter to match the outside thread diameter of the die. For example, to cut a ¼–20 thread, the diameter of the work must be exactly ¼".

The threads are beveled slightly on one side of the die to make starting easier and to form the thread gradually. Always begin by inserting the beveled side onto the end of the stock. Grasp the die stock (the die holder) with both hands and press firmly while slowly turning it clockwise. When the threads have started it will no longer be necessary to press down. As in tapping, back off after each turn to break and clear the chips.

6 | Edge Finishing

All sawed edges of acrylics will have distinctive tool marks or ripples—some relatively smooth, others rough, depending upon the characteristics of the tool used. Scribed-and-broken edges are comparatively smooth, with the exception of a narrow band in the area in which the scriber has penetrated the surface. Here the edges will be slightly dulled because of the scraping action of the scribing tool. Another characteristic of the scribed edge is that it will be very slightly but definitely beveled in the area that was scored because of the tapered cross section of the tool, which actually scrapes a V-shaped groove.

Regardless of the method used to cut the material, additional hand or machine operations are necessary to eliminate the marks, to correct cutting irregularities, to true edges for making good cemented joints, and to obtain finished edges. You can restore the edges to a smooth, a satin-translucent, or a high-gloss transparent finish by filing, scraping, sanding, and buffing. The last, buffing, is employed only to achieve transparency.

FILING. Fine-tooth files can be used to smooth out tool marks and for general stock removal in order to shape or true an edge. Medium and coarse files are only for heavy stock removal.

You can handle practically any job with a set of four basic file shapes: flat, half-round, triangular, and round. The flat file is for straight work and outside curves, while the half-round handles inside curves. The triangular file is for small tight corners, and the round (or rattail) serves for small holes and small curves. Files are relatively inexpensive so if you want to add two more useful ones to the collection, you might consider a knife file for cleaning out acute angles, corners, or slots, and a safe-edge that has one or two sides smooth or uncut, thus permitting filing up to an inside corner without danger of cutting into the adjoining surface. Since metal chips wedged between file teeth can scratch acrylic, it is advisable to reserve a set of files for plastics use only.

Secure the work firmly in a vise, using wood pads to protect the surface if the jaws are metal. Hold the file with two hands and apply an even downward pressure on the forward stroke only. Avoid a rocking motion unless a rounded edge is desired. For most operations the file should be pushed straight ahead or slightly diagonally across the work. For a finer finish on flat work, try draw-filing: Grasp the file at each end and with an even pressure alternately push and pull the file while keeping it perpendicular to the direction of motion.

Filing a surface sufficiently true for a good cement joint requires a bit of practice, but until you acquire the skill you can use a simple trick to get it right. Clamp the work in the vise sandwiched between two pieces of hardwood about ¾" thick and extending a few inches beyond the ends of the workpiece. Align the three so the edge of the plastic projects very slightly above the level of the wood, then draw-file the entire length of the pack. The wood shoulders will guide the file accurately lengthwise and crosswise. If a number of thin pieces of stock are involved, they can be ganged together to save time and effort.

Filing is especially effective for leveling high spots, rounding corners, and smoothing uneven cuts, but the operation sometimes can be bypassed. If the edge is relatively even and in need only of trueing and smoothing, you can go directly from cutting to scraping.

SCRAPING. Cutting-tool marks as well as new ones sometimes introduced by filing are easily removed by scraping the edge with any one of a variety of tools. You can use a cabinet scraper, a plane blade, a chisel, or even the back of a hacksaw blade which has been ground flat. Or you may opt to purchase an edge-scraping tool which can be used for acrylic sheets up to ½" thick. This tool has a right-angle lip which rides the surface of the sheet, thus assuring a true, square cut.

A cabinet scraper or modified hacksaw blade must be ground square without a burr or wire edge. Use an oilstone after grinding or filing to obtain the necessary clean edge.

Square-edged tools should be held at an angle of about 45° to the surface, while sharp-edged tools such as the chisel or plane blade should be held straight up, perpendicular to the surface.

This inexpensive tool enables you to scrape an edge to a true right angle.

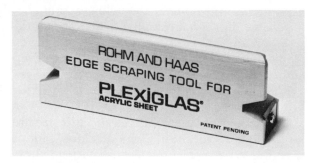

Gang-scraping several edges at one time with a chisel. This method saves time and promotes accuracy.

To scrape an edge, secure the work in a vise, grasp the tool firmly with both hands, then, starting at the far end, draw it toward you in one continuous pass. If the tool is sharp and the pressure even, the shavings will come off in long ribbons. For best results make several light passes rather than fewer heavy ones. Too heavy a hand may cause the tool to dig in and skip, resulting in tool marks you hadn't bargained for. Holding a sharp-edged tool at an angle greater than 90° (with the handle tilted back) will cause the same problem. Take special care when scraping parts for solvent-cement joints, because flat surfaces are essential.

Bevels and sanding-ready rounded edges can also be formed by scraping. To make a bevel, draw the tool over the edge at a constant angle to remove as much of the edge corner as required. To rough-round an edge, scrape with a series of ever-changing angles.

For applications such as window glazing where a fine finished edge is not required, sharp corners should be eased by scraping a slight bevel. Crude saw marks left in such an edge make the material very crack-sensitive under impact.

SANDING. Acrylics may be sanded by hand or with a variety of power sanders. The belt, disk, and drum sanders are effective for stock removal in shaping and trueing and for preliminary fine finishing. In many cases these tools will obviate the filing operation. However, a collection of power sanders is not essential to do good work—they only speed it along.

When an edge has been scraped it will have a fairly smooth, dull matte appearance which will require sanding to prepare it for cementing or to give it a final finish. Since the scraped edge is relatively smooth to begin with, only a minimal amount of sanding will usually be necessary to bring it to a fine finish.

The type of coated abrasives and grit size are important considerations in sanding acrylics. Flint, the original "sandpaper," is too soft and fast-wearing to be of any practical use with acrylics. Garnet is harder than flint and is frequently used but is superseded in hardness by aluminum oxide. And still harder is silicon carbide, which is available with a waterproof backing. Usually simply refered to as "wet-or-dry," this abrasive can be used with water as a lubricant to produce an extremely smooth surface. Because of the higher cost of silicon carbide abrasives, aluminum oxide is recommended for general sanding and the wet-or-dry for fine finishing.

Grit size. Grit or grain sizes of abrasives range from a very coarse 12 to extremely fine 600. The number indicates the quantity of grains per inch if laid end to end. The relative roughness or smoothness of the cutting action and the amount of stock removed are directly proportional to grain size. As a rule, sanding should start with an abrasive just coarse enough to remove previous marks on the material or to shape the surface with a minimum of roughness. Progressively finer grits are used to improve the surface until the desired finish is obtained. Grits coarser than 80 are rarely used on acrylics. A typical progression from rough sanding to satin finish would be, for example, 80, 120, 220, 320, and 360 grit. Starting from a scraped edge the sequence would perhaps begin with 220 or 320 grit, depending on the keenness of the scraping tool used. Skipping intermediate grades simply necessitates more effort with the next-finer grade to remove the previous grade's "scratches." It should be noted that power sanding does permit skipping grades. Also, for a given grit, power sanding will produce a smoother finish than will hand sanding.

Disk sander. The stationary disk sander can be used for trueing straight ends of stock which are a bit smaller in dimension than the radius of the disk. Work which is wider would extend to the center, where very little cutting action occurs as compared to the outside of the disk, which, in effect, is turning faster. The stock should continually be moved back and forth to prevent overheating and to equalize the cut. You can feed the work freehand, but a miter gauge will help to obtain greater accuracy. Tilt the table to sand a bevel or chamfer. This sander is especially useful for rounding corners or for sanding outside curves of unlimited radius.

The disk sander excels for trueing small edges. Move the work continually to equalize the cut—the center turns slower than the outside.

Belt sander. The belt sander is more versatile than the disk sander. It can perform the same functions as the disk, and more. It does a better job on end sanding because the rotation of the belt is uniform across its entire width. Also, because of the length of the belt, heat is more readily dissipated.

With the sanding table adjusted to the vertical position, you can easily handle outside curves. Tilt the work table to sand bevels and chamfers. Sand inside curves on the end drum.

Sanding drum. Sanding drums of various sizes are used to sand the edges of holes and irregular shapes which include both inside and outside curves. You can attach them to a portable drill, a drill press, or directly to a motor shaft.

Due to the relatively small surface area, excessive speed should be avoided to prevent overheating. Usually, 1,800 rpm works well with acrylics, but do a test on scrap. If scorching occurs, you may need a lighter pressure, a lower speed, or both.

Most work can be done freehand, but uneven feed pressure or unintentional hesitation at any one spot will cause the drum to dig in, causing an indent in the work.

Hand sanding. Because of the tendency of extra-fine abrasives to clog and overheat, fine edge finishing can be troublesome on stationary sanding equipment. Therefore this operation is usually best done with a portable finishing sander or by hand.

Hand sanding should be done with the abrasive paper firmly backed up with a wood block, a rubber or felt pad, or shaped sticks. A hard backup will result in a flat edge, while the softer materials will produce a slightly rounded "soft" edge. The latter is usually preferred for most projects.

For sanding small holes or curves, you can wrap the abrasive paper around a dowel or a cardboard tube, with or without a soft padding, depending on the result you want. Round stock can best be sanded with a strip of cloth-backed abrasive manipulated in the manner of a shoeshine

Hand-sanding small pieces. Place the abrasive on a flat surface and move the work in a circular motion.

rag. You can tear the abrasive into very narrow strips and use the same procedure to get into very tight spaces. To sand small pieces or the ends of rods and tubes, put a sheet of abrasive paper on a perfectly flat surface. Hold the stock firmly and rub it briskly over the abrasive surface.

SATIN FINISH. A frosted satin finish is achieved by wet sanding with wet-or-dry paper using progressively finer papers up to 320 or 360 grit. Parts which are to be cement-joined are sanded to this stage. Be careful to avoid rounding the edges, as this will result in poor contact in the cemented joint.

Secure the part in the vise and back the abrasive paper with a wood block. Dip the paper in water frequently to float off particles and to reduce friction. Make firm continuous passes along the entire edge. Wipe the surface dry with a tissue to check the progress—the wet surface will always appear glossy.

A finishing sander should never be used for edges which are to be cemented, because the resilient felt backup pad will cause slight rounding of the edges, but it can be used to finish exposed edges. Ordinary sanders are not designed to be immersed in water, so this should *never* be done, but you can brush some water onto the edge of the work.

When sanding exposed edges by hand, use a rubber or felt pad attached to the wood block for straight work or outside curves but eliminate the wood block for inside curves. Always ease sharp corners of exposed edges by making a few angled passes over them.

If a still-finer finish is desired, continue sanding with 360 grit, but don't go any further, as the edge will begin to lose its satin translucency.

TRANSPARENT FINISH. To obtain a high-gloss transparent edge, continue sanding with 400, 500, and 600 grit. This is followed by buffing, which can be done by hand or with a power buffing wheel.

A 6- or 8-inch muslin wheel driven by a 1,750-rpm motor is ideal for polishing, but if you don't have this equipment a 3- or 4-inch wheel at-

Power buffing quickly produces a high-gloss transparent edge. Use the highest speed available and a moderate pressure.

When using a stationary buffer, feed the work slightly below center of wheel and move it back and forth.

tached to a portable drill will do. A buffing kit which includes a stick of buffing compound is usually available where acrylics are sold. Since the final touch requires a few passes with a clean dry cotton flannel wheel, a second buff should be on hand. However, you can do the dry rub by hand with a cloth in lieu of a second wheel.

Charge the wheel with a bit of compound. Tripoli, gray or white buffing compound is recommended. Hold the work firmly and apply only moderate pressure, keeping the wheel (or the work) constantly moving to prevent overheating. Compound deposited on the work indicates too much pressure or too much compound. This should be avoided. If a wheel is overloaded with compound or is caked with dry lumps of it, run it against a fine-tooth sawblade to remove the deposit.

When working with a stationary wheel it should turn overhand toward you. Edge work should be applied in the lower quadrant, never above center.

Hand buffing.   This is not at all difficult and will produce a finish equal to that achieved with power buffing.

The buffing compounds used with power wheels are too dry for use in hand buffing. A product such as DuPont Auto Polishing Compound (not the rubbing compound) works exceptionally well. Ordinary toothpaste—not the gel type—also works well. Apply the paste to a piece of water-dampened felt or short-nap carpeting attached to a block of wood. The wood backup is not used for irregular contours. Rub the surface briskly until it sparkles, then finish off with a clean dry cloth. The edges of holes or other shapes which cannot be readily buffed in this manner can be done with a piece of terrycloth charged with compound and rubbed shoeshine-fashion. A piece of string can be used for small corners.

Deep holes.   Deep holes which do not go completely through the material are somewhat difficult to polish by buffing, but the problem is easily solved with solvent polishing.

Clean out the hole of any lubricant residue which may have been left after drilling, then fill the hole with solvent cement. Let it stand for about 30 seconds, then pour it off. (Care must be taken not to get solvent on the surface of the sheet, as it will blush and mar it. It's safer to flush with water to dilute the solvent.) Allow the work to stand overnight until the softened wall of the hole hardens.

7 | Heat Forming

Formability is one of the most useful properties of acrylic as a crafting material. Since it is thermoplastic, it becomes soft and pliable when heated to forming temperatures between 290° and 340° F. While in this elastic state the material can be formed into many different shapes. Upon cooling it becomes rigid and retains the shape to which it has been formed.

Forming acrylic sheet is by far the simplest type of fabrication. It permits making three-dimensional shapes while bypassing three basic operations. Consider, for example, the need for a right-angle corner in a project. By heating a narrow band of a flat sheet, a 90° bend can readily be made to form the corner. The alternative method would require cutting the sheet into two pieces, finishing the edges, then cementing. Angled joints other than 45° are considerably more demanding to fabricate by cutting and cementing, whereas a change in plane from 1° all the way to 180° is possible by heat forming.

Acrylic has another advantageous property—elastic memory. When a formed part is reheated to the forming temperature, it will revert back into its original flat-sheet condition. Thus errors in forming can be corrected by reheating and reforming.

There are two methods you can utilize in the home or shop: strip heat forming and drape forming. Both procedures carried out as described are simple and quite safe. It should be noted that acrylic plastic is a slow-burning combustible material and will ignite at temperatures of about 700° F. Therefore open flame should never be used to heat it. Nor should it ever be heated in a kitchen oven. The ordinary home oven is not equipped with adequate temperature control nor proper venting. Monomer bleed-off gases emitted by heated plastic and trapped in the enclosed space could explode.

The protective masking paper must be removed before the plastic is heated so it is important to carry out the edge-finishing operations before forming, while the paper is intact. Heating masked material will ruin the paper adhesive and make it impossible to remove.

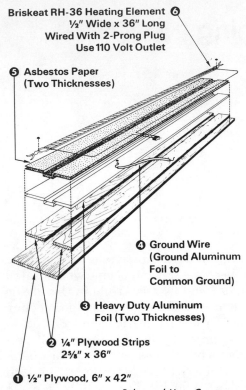

Briskeat RH-36 Heating Element ❻
½" Wide x 36" Long
Wired With 2-Prong Plug
Use 110 Volt Outlet

❺ Asbestos Paper
(Two Thicknesses)

❹ Ground Wire
(Ground Aluminum
Foil to
Common Ground)

❸ Heavy Duty Aluminum
Foil (Two Thicknesses)

❷ ¼" Plywood Strips
2⅝" x 36"

❶ ½" Plywood, 6" x 42"

Exploded view of strip heater.

Rohm and Haas Company

MAKING A STRIP HEATER.
The easiest way to bend acrylic along a straight line is with the use of a strip heater, which provides controlled local heat in the area to be bent.

Strip heaters are commercially available but tend to be quite costly. You can build your own at low cost with a special heating element which is available where acrylics are sold. The materials required include: plywood, heavy-duty aluminum foil, asbestos paper, a length of ground wire, and a Briskeat RH-36 Heating Element. Proceed as follows.

Cut a piece of ½" plywood 6" ×42" and two pieces of ¼" plywood 2⅝" × 36". Nail the ¼" strips onto the ½" base, centered lengthwise, leaving a ¾" channel along the center.

Cut two pieces of aluminum foil 6" × 36" and fold into the channel and over the strips. Attach the ground wire to the foil with a panhead screw. This wire should be long enough to reach a common ground, such as the coverplate screw on an electrical outlet (this protects against shock in the event of a short circuit).

Cut two pieces of asbestos paper (available at hardware stores) 6¼" × 36". (Asbestos particles are dangerous, but in paper form it is rather firm and not subject to pulverization, provided it is cut with a sharp knife so that clean edges are obtained.) Place this over the foil and fold it neatly into the channel, then staple it along the outer edges of the plywood strips. Asbestos paper is brittle and tends to break when folded, but this can be prevented by dampening the paper down the center where it fits into the channel in the center of the heater base.

Lay the heating element in the channel and drive a nail 1½″ from each end of the base to permit tying the attachment strings which are on the ends of the heating element.

With the ground wire connected and the unit plugged into a 110-volt outlet, a safe maximum forming temperature is quickly reached. This heater is suitable for forming material up to ¼″ thick.

Making straight-line bends.   Plug in the heater several minutes before use to get it up to maximum temperature. Remove the masking paper from the plastic sheet, then mark the bend line with a Blaisdell china-marking pencil. This brand will not scratch or stain the surface when heated, and the mark can readily be removed afterward by wiping with a cloth.

Place the sheet on the heater so the area to be bent is directly over the heating element. If the sheet is not marked with a bend line it can be positioned by measuring with a rule. The sheet should not touch the heating element, and it won't if the unit was properly constructed with the element taut and resting flat on the bottom of the channel.

Allow the material to heat thoroughly before bending to avoid stress-crazing (internal cracks). The surface will develop a slight welt when the time is right for bending. This will usually take about 4 to 6 minutes for ⅛″ stock and between 12 to 15 minutes for ¼″ material. Overheating can cause scorching and bubbling, so it must be avoided. You will find a timer helpful to eliminate guesswork once you have established correct timings for your particular heater with materials of various thicknesses. Careful timing is also important to ensure that all similar bends will have the same

Allow the plastic to heat until it welts slightly, then make the bend away from the heated side. Time all similar bends to obtain same radii. Wood block guides right-angle bend here.

radius, because within limitations, the softer the state of the plastic, the larger the resulting radius.

If the work extends beyond the sides of the heater, prop up the over-hanging portions so they won't tip down as the material softens. Otherwise the heated section will rise away from the heat.

Bends are made away from the heated side; to do otherwise will cause stress-crazing and wrinkling. Freehand bends frequently will do, but when exacting results are required some form of guide will be necessary. This could be simply a square, a block of wood, or a full-size drawing against which to make the bend.

Problem solving.   When only a portion of a sheet requires bending, use a heat shield under those areas which are to remain cool. Thin layers of asbestos paper or aluminum foil can be used to effectively block off the heat.

A bend with a greater radius than that which results with normal strip heating can be made by continually shifting the work over the heating element to heat a wider area of the sheet.

The rule of making the bend away from the heated side sometimes must be broken in order to achieve bends in opposite directions on two different planes. When this cannot be avoided the "wrong" bend should be made on the least conspicuous section of the work so that stress-crazing or wrinkling which may occur will be less prominent. (Wrong-side bends are generally not a problem for bends of 90° or less.) The alternative would be to use a cemented joint in combination with the heat-formed fabrica-tion.

When a project requires several bends with the ends of the pre-cut sheet meeting at a specific location, it is sometimes difficult to predict the final result beforehand because of the slight dimensional change that occurs in bending. A test bending with a narrow strip of scrap stock of the same thickness as the workpiece will prove useful for working out the dimen-sions before the actual workpiece is cut to size and marked for bending.

DRAPE FORMING.   The drape forming of sizable workpieces necessi-tates heating the entire sheet in a special oven designed for the purpose. Since the kitchen oven is not a suitable heat source for the reason given earlier, drape forming in the home shop should be limited to relatively small workpieces or small sections of larger ones. The usual source of heat is a heat lamp or a flameless heat gun.

To shape the plastic, first place it over a form of the desired shape. When sufficiently heated until it becomes limp, the material drapes itself over the form and retains the shape after cooling. (See the Mondrian Table project in Chapter 10.)

Heat guns usually produce intense heat in temperature ranges which are too high for use on acrylics unless great care is exercised to avoid scorching or burning. However, reduced-heat accessory nozzles are available for these devices and should be used for safe working. The heat lamp doesn't deliver quite as much heat as the gun, but it too must be handled carefully to avoid overheating problems.

Test either of these heat sources on scrap before use on actual work in order to learn the dos and don'ts. Always work in a well-ventilated area and have a general-purpose ABC-rated (dry-powder) fire extinguisher nearby. This applies for strip-heating operations as well.

Forms can be made of a variety of materials, including wood, metal, and sheet laminates. Whatever material you use, its surface should be smooth. When a sheet of acrylic is heated to forming temperature its softened surface will be indented by any irregularities present on the form surface. The transferred imperfection, called "mark-off," can ruin a piece of work. Softwood such as pine is generally used to make forms because it is so easy to work. Its contact surfaces must be smooth-sanded, however, if mark-off is to be avoided.

When the heated material has fully draped over the form, it must be held in place while it cools, or some springback will occur. You can do this with rubber bands, tape, clamps, or your hands (wear gloves).

Because of the concentrated heat pattern of the heat sources, both types should be moved constantly over the entire area involved in order to obtain uniform heating. Stock up to ¼" thick can be formed into compound curves, but heavier material up to ½" thick will be limited to large-radius straight bends only up to about several inches in length unless more than one heat source is used. Whenever possible, thick material should be heated from both sides.

8 | Joining the Parts

Acrylic parts are bonded in two ways to form permanent transparent joints: with solvent cement or with thickened solvent cement.

SOLVENT CEMENT.   The easiest and most convenient way to join acrylic to acrylic is by capillary-action cementing using a solvent such as methylene chloride. This is a clear, watery fluid usually simply called MDC, available at plastics-supply outlets.

The solvent is not a cement in the sense that it has any adhesive properties per se. It simply has the ability to dissolve and soften acrylic plastic. When it is applied to mating surfaces, fusion occurs at the interface of the joints. As the solvent evaporates (in 15 to 20 seconds) the surfaces harden to form a solid bond.

If two mating surfaces are very well matched, solvent introduced at the joint line will quickly spread throughout the joint area by capillary action, a phenomenon of surface tension. It is for this reason that an edge prepared for cementing must be perfectly flat without even the slightest rounding or other irregularity. A joint which is not matched will be mottled and pocked with tiny air voids (bubbles) as a result of uneven dispersion of the solvent. Such a joint will be unsound as well as unattractive.

When you doubt the integrity of a joint, you can pretest it by wetting the surface with water. The film of water will spread out evenly when a good joint is pressed together. Disassemble and dry thoroughly before cementing.

To cement a joint, remove the masking paper, then dry-assemble the pieces, using masking tape or simple wood jigs to hold them together with moderate pressure. Excessive pressure is not necessary or desirable.

The solvent may be applied with a fine brush, with an eye dropper, or, for the best results, with a special solvent applicator which can be purchased at moderate cost. The applicator consists of a plastic squeeze bottle with an extremely fine metal nozzle which permits a very neat, controlled application, quick and easy.

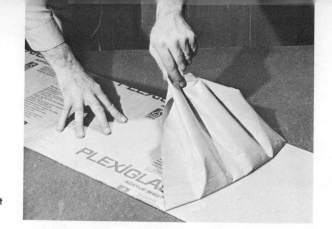

Remove the protective masking only after all machining and finishing operations have been completed. Remove all dust particles before assembly.

It is important to position the assembly so that the joint interface is in a horizontal plane. Capillary action will draw the solvent into the joint. If the joint is in the vertical plane, gravity will cause most of the solvent to run out the bottom before it has a chance to be fully effective, and it will also damage the surface of the material. Whenever possible the solvent should be applied to both sides of the joint.

When a fully enclosed hollow construction is to be cemented, a vent should be provided, if feasible, to allow the solvent vapors to escape. Entrapped vapors could cause crazing.

The setting time may vary from a few seconds to a half hour or longer, depending upon the cement used and the ambient temperature in the workroom. Higher temperatures promote faster setting. Acrylic should not be cemented at temperatures below 65° F.

Occasionally a project design may require cementing a heat-formed edge to a flat sheet. Inspection of the formed edge will reveal a slight bulge in the area of the bend. This must be filed and/or sanded flush before you attempt to make a cemented joint.

Rohm and Haas Company

Masking tape is used to assemble the parts for cementing. Note that all exposed edges have been polished; joint edges are satin-finished.

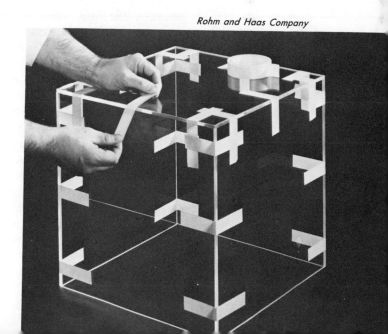

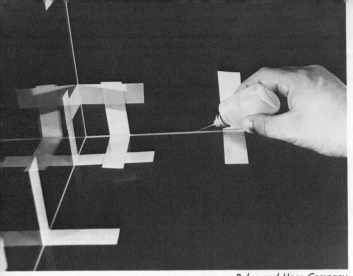

Solvent cement is applied to joint with special applicator. Capillary action draws the fluid into the joint. Joint face must be in horizontal plane for good results.

Rohm and Haas Company

THICKENED SOLVENT CEMENT. Thickened cement is usually a formulation of methylene chloride with acrylic polymer added. It is used to produce stronger joints with exceptionally good outdoor weatherability. Because of its viscosity, thickened cement is advantageous for use on joints which are somewhat less than good-fitting. It will fill gaps within reasonable limits.

Thickened cement is available in squeeze tubes as well as in bulk. Weld-On #16 is a widely used product. A small bead is applied to one edge of the joint. The parts are brought together gently, then clamped or held firmly until they set. The joint must be allowed to cure for about two hours before handling. Care must be exercised to avoid overapplication of cement, because the squeeze-out will be difficult to remove once hardened.

When you want to join two edges, side by side, you cannot use solvent cement successfully because the joint would be in a vertical plane, and thus the solvent would pass through and run out the bottom. On the other hand, if you positioned the joint in a horizontal plane, much of the solvent would run down the side of the work, resulting in a starved joint and a marred side. The remedy is to use thickened cement.

The parts are positioned side by side on two boards, which are spaced apart slightly under the joint line. The gap allows the squeezed-out cement to drop away, clear of the work. If this precaution is not taken the bottom surfaces would be smeared with cement and seriously marred. (The procedure is illustrated for the Étagère project in Chapter 10.)

Thickened cement is useful for making repairs and for filling in scratches. Deep scratches may require several applications with 24 hours drying time in between.

Caution: Solvents may be toxic if inhaled for extended periods of time or if swallowed; many are also flammable. Work with solvents and cements only in a well-ventilated room, and make certain that no vapor can reach an open flame or other source of ignition.

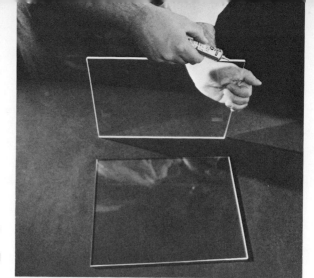

Thickened cement is used to make a very strong, weatherproof joint. Owing to its viscosity, it is especially effective on imperfectly fitted joints as it fills small gaps.

Rohm and Haas Company

BONDING ACRYLIC TO OTHER MATERIALS. Good bonds between acrylics and metal, wood, glass, and other materials may be obtained with the use of a variety of adhesives. Because of the different coefficients of thermal expansion of acrylics and other materials, a general rule is to select an adhesive that will remain somewhat elastic. Contact cement and many of the paneling adhesives work quite well, but of course they are not transparent and therefore they cannot be used for see-through applications.

Epoxies bond very well but do set quite hard. Therefore when large areas are involved a buffer of cork or rubber is generally recommended between the two surfaces to be joined.

When using acrylic glazing, you should allow an expansion space between the plastic and the framing. A flexible compound such as silicone sealant or acrylic caulking compound should be used to seal the joint.

Epoxy is good for joining acrylic to wood. Quick-setting type is best because it minimizes run-off.

9 | Engraving

Make a scratch on the surface of a sheet of transparent acrylic with a sharp knife and you'll note that the line will be bright in contrast to the clear surrounding area, because its dull surface reflects light. This is the basis of surface etching or engraving, a means of decorating plastic projects or of creating decorative pieces which will stand on their own merit.

The technique is not difficult; in its simplest form it merely involves tracing over a drawing with a knife to etch an image in a sheet of clear plastic. Or it can be done freehand for originality. More advanced deeper engraving can be done with rotary burrs using a hand grinder or a flexible-shaft power source.

KNIFE ENGRAVING. A hobby craft knife, such as an X-acto, with two blades, a slender point and a quarter-round, will do fine.

Select an illustration which has easy-to-follow lines for a start. Lay the sheet of plastic over it and tape the picture along one edge. This will permit lifting the plastic away to check progress without losing alignment. Grasp the knife as you would a pencil (it has basically the same shape) and press firmly to scratch the surface following the outlines of the illustration. Short lines can be made in continuous sweeps; long ones are made in sections to permit repositioning the knife to a sidewise scraping attitude. When continuing a long line after a stop, avoid starting where you left off. Instead, back up in the existing line slightly, then continue. The result will be a smoother blend.

The slender blade is used for main outlining; the quarter-round is used for shading. Regardless of the blade used, the knife should be angled slightly toward the direction of travel in order to obtain a smooth scraping action.

POWER ENGRAVING. A small assortment of engraving cutters chucked into a high-speed power source are used to obtain cuts with

A simple double-panel knife etching. The fish appears to move when the viewer's head moves sideways because of the displacement of the images.

greater depth and variety than can be accomplished with a knife. The Dremel Moto-Tool hand grinder is an excellent tool for the purpose.

Cutters for this tool are available in a variety of shapes and sizes. For a start you can get by with a few, including the ball, pear, cone, and end mill shapes. The ball is used for general outlining—a small one for thin lines, a large one for broad lines. The pear is used to produce a teardrop shape. The cone is used to obtain a triangular pattern, and the end mill for radial slits. There are no set rules concerning which cutter to use for the job at hand. Choice is a matter of personal preference, which develops through experience. Practice on scrap to get the feel of handling the tool and to learn what each cutter can do.

Engraving can be done from above or below the sheet of plastic. Working from the bottom will enable you to see the progress of the work more

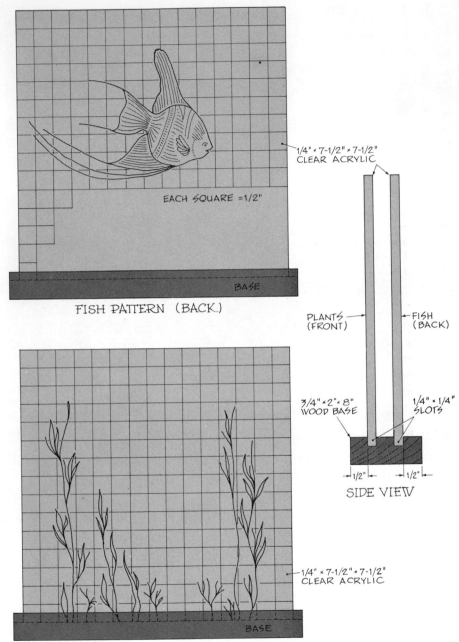

EACH SQUARE =1/2"

FISH PATTERN (BACK)

BASE

1/4" × 7-1/2" × 7-1/2"
CLEAR ACRYLIC

PLANTS
(FRONT)

FISH
(BACK)

3/4" × 2" × 8"
WOOD BASE

1/4" × 1/4"
SLOTS

1/2"   1/2"

SIDE VIEW

PLANT PATTERN (FRONT)

BASE

1/4" × 7-1/2" × 7-1/2"
CLEAR ACRYLIC

The image is etched with a sharp-pointed knife following the drawing taped to the bottom of the plastic sheet. The round blade is used for shading.

clearly, but the technique is somewhat more difficult to master than the topside approach. In either case the tool must be held firmly to prevent the cutter from running across the surface like a wheel. You can work freehand if you have a talent for drawing. If not, draw the design on the back side of the sheet with a fine-pointed china marker.

Lift the plastic away from the drawing to check the progress of the work.

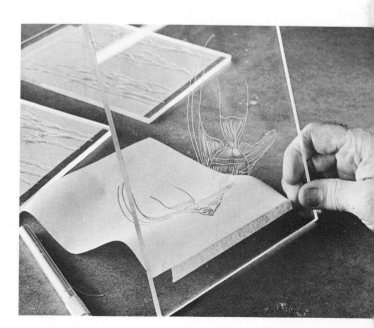

This image was made with a small ball-shaped cutter in a Moto-Tool hand grinder.

PLAN

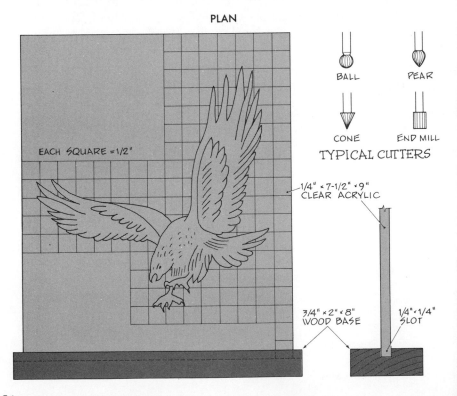

EACH SQUARE = 1/2"

BALL

PEAR

CONE

END MILL

TYPICAL CUTTERS

1/4" × 7-1/2" × 9"
CLEAR ACRYLIC

3/4" × 2" × 8"
WOOD BASE

1/4" × 1/4"
SLOT

Tape the drawing to the bottom of the plastic sheet, then trace over the lines with a china marker sharpened to a fine point.

Turn the sheet over and rest one end on a piece of wood to prevent marring the drawn image. Hold the tool firmly and simply make light passes over the image.

EDGE LIGHTING.   Since engraving only scratches the surface, relatively thin stock can be used for the purpose of obtaining an image. However, the brightness of the image is proportional to the amount of light entering the edge of the material. Given the same intensity of edge illumination, an image on ¼" stock will be brighter than the same image on ⅛" stock.

Engraved images stand out quite well under normal illumination, but when edge-lighted with a concealed light source they become luminous, more brilliant and quite striking. Engravings which are made for the express purpose of being edge-lighted should have a flat, highly polished edge at the light source in order to obtain high illumination through the sheet. To further intensify the illumination the edge opposite the light-source edge should be painted flat white. This will reflect light back into the scene.

To make a very interesting display piece you might try this novel approach: Engrave images on two or three separate sheets of plastic and dye the bottom edges of each with a different color. Stand them slightly separated in a boxed base which contains a light bulb. The image on each sheet will glow with an individual color, and the overall effect will be a multicolored scene.

Another idea is to engrave a single sheet which is then dyed with different colors on two opposite edges. When illuminated from both edges the image will accent the color nearest the particular edge and will be a blend of both colors in the center area. Dyes for acrylics can be obtained at plastics dealers.

Note that light boxes made for edge-lighted displays should be well vented and the bulb must be spaced far enough away from the acrylic edge to prevent overheating.

10 | Acrylic Projects

The procedures just discussed cover the basics of working with acrylics. The next step in developing your skills is to build a few projects and learn by doing.

The projects in this chapter were selected because they include a well-rounded variety of operations. If any appeal to you, you're on your way as soon as you obtain the necessary materials.

Otherwise, let the projects serve as a guide; you can modify them to suit your personal likes or you may wish to start from scratch with concepts of your own.

FOLD-OUT SHELVES. For a refreshing departure from the ordinary fabrication methods used with conventional materials such as wood, try your hand with heat-formed foldout techniques. The procedure will enable you to shape flat sheet into an unlimited variety of interesting configurations. This series of novel curio-shelf designs illustrates the possibilities.

Two of the units are fabricated from single sheets of acrylic; the patterns are cut out in the flat, then variously bent, through heating, to form the desired shape. The hex-shaped unit is also essentially a heat-formed construction but it differs from the others in that it cannot be unfolded from a single sheet. The upper half of the hex must be formed separately, then joined by solvent cementing.

All the shelves illustrated are made with 3/16" Plexiglas sheet in varied transparent colors, including amber, red, and yellow. They can, of course, be made with clear colorless sheet for an equally striking effect.

A table saw equipped with a small-diameter fine-tooth plywood blade is ideal for making the straight cuts, but a saber saw will also do. Note that some of the layouts require internal cuts. You can accomplish these cuts almost to completion by manipulating the blade-elevating feature of the machine, as described in Chapter 4 on cutting.

Hexagonal curio shelf in amber acrylic is an eye-catcher.

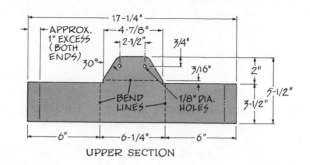

UPPER SECTION

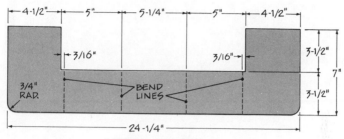

LOWER SECTION

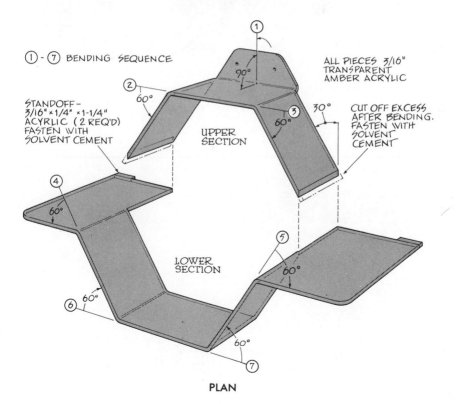

PLAN

One-piece foldout shelf executed in transparent red acrylic.

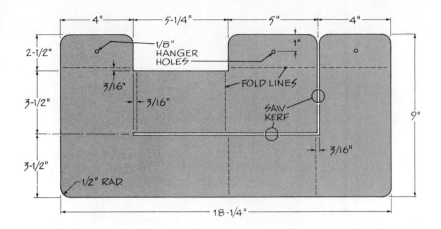

4" 5-1/4" 5" 4"

2-1/2"

1/8" HANGER HOLES

1"

3/16"

3/16"

FOLD LINES

SAW KERF

3-1/2"

9"

3/16"

3-1/2"

1/2" RAD.

18-1/4"

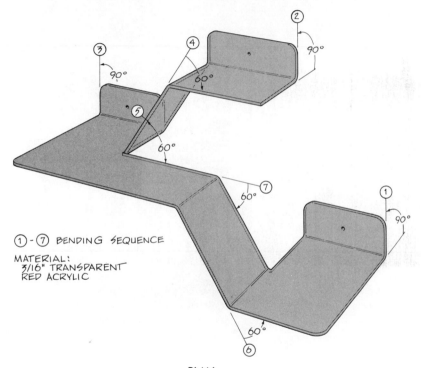

②
90°

③
90°

④
60°

⑤

60°

60°

⑦

60°

①
90°

①-⑦ BENDING SEQUENCE

MATERIAL:
3/16" TRANSPARENT
RED ACRYLIC

60°
⑥

PLAN

61

One-piece foldout ladder shelf in clear golden yellow is the simplest one to make.

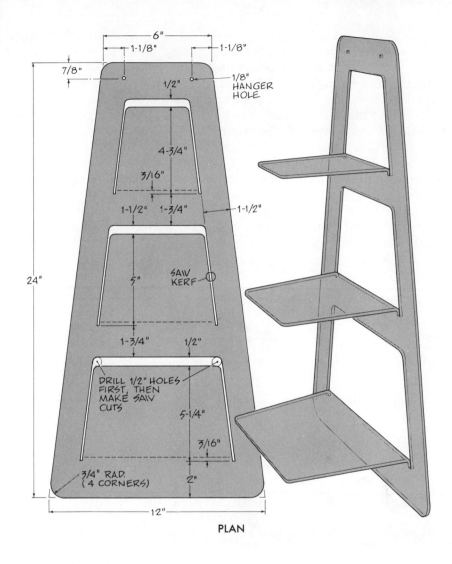

6"

1-1/8"   1-1/8"

7/8"

1/8"
HANGER
HOLE

1/2"

4-3/4"

3/16"

1-1/2"   1-3/4"   1-1/2"

24"

5"   SAW
       KERF

1-3/4"   1/2"

DRILL 1/2" HOLES
FIRST, THEN
MAKE SAW
CUTS

5-1/4"

3/16"

3/4" RAD.   2"
(4 CORNERS)

12"

PLAN

Scrape, sand, and polish all the edges which are accessible before beginning the forming operations. There is one exception: The ends of the hex section which are joined by cementing must remain unpolished.

When all machining is carried out as far as possible, remove the masking paper and mark the bending lines as indicated, using a china-marking pencil. Place the sheet on the strip heater and allow the plastic to heat thoroughly until it welts slightly along the line.

For some bending it will be necessary to heat only part of the sheet. This is done by using a few thicknesses of asbestos paper between the heating element and the portions which are to be kept unheated. Be sure to follow the bending sequences indicated in the drawings.

The upper half section of the hex formation is cut a few inches longer than the required finished size, then bent and marked for sawing the ends at angles to fit snug against the lower section's edges.

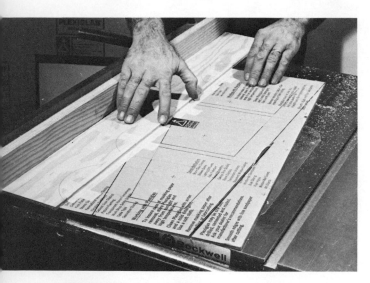

Tapered sides of one-piece fold-out shelf are ripped with the aid of a taped-on board which guides the workpiece past the blade at the required angle. Tape securely on both sides.

Inside-corner radius is formed by drilling a ½" hole at each location.

Begin edge finishing by scraping. Use two hands for this (one hand is used here for photo clarity). Follow by sanding and polishing. Inside edges are finished after folding.

Inside cuts on table saw are made by cranking the rotating blade up through the work.

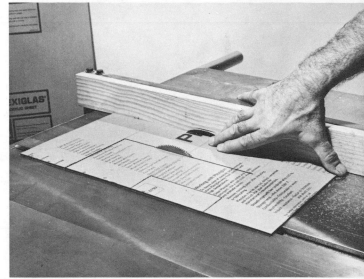

The area to be bent is centered over the heating element and gently folded when sufficiently softened. Note how strips of asbestos paper are used to keep heat from parts which are not to be bent.

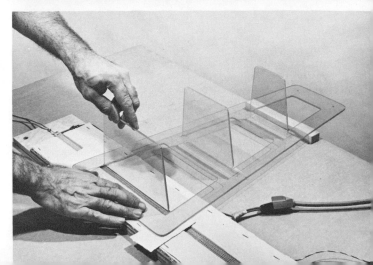

Bending the half section of the hex. Masking has been only partially removed so the ends will be protected later during angle cutoff operation. T bevel is used to check angles.

The beveled edges of hex shelf are taped to the lower section and solvent-cemented.

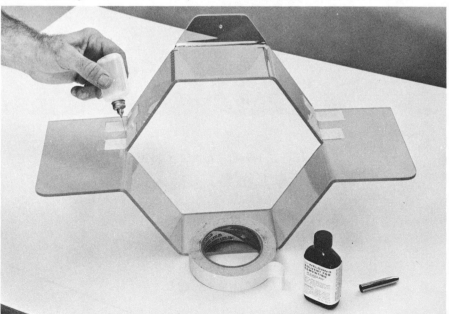

XMAS TREE.   A sheet of clear colorless ¼" acrylic and pressure-sensitive prismatic foil is used to make this novel accessory. The foil, generally used for auto-body decorating, is available at many auto-supply stores.

Use a coping or saber saw to cut the outline of the tree. The slip joint in the base must fit snug, so it is advisable to cut the slots slightly undersize. They can then be carefully filed to size for a good-fitting joint.

Use a hacksaw blade with the back edge ground to sharp corners to scrape the edges free of saw ripples. Sand the edges smooth, finishing off with wet-or-dry paper lubricated with water. Use a piece of cloth charged with auto polishing compound or toothpaste and rub in shoeshine fashion to obtain a highly polished finish.

The foil "ornaments" can be cut with scissors or they can be formed with variously sized clicker or saddler's punches available at hardware and leathercraft dealers.

The prismatic-foil ornaments on this acrylic Christmas tree sparkle in every color of the spectrum as light strikes their many facets.

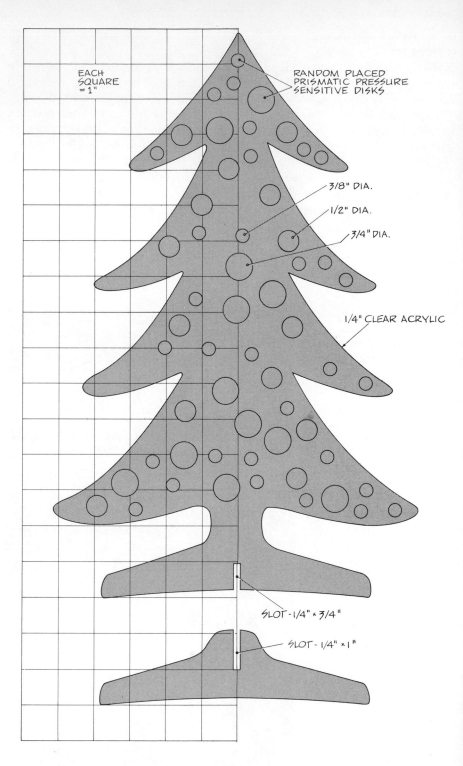

EACH SQUARE = 1"

RANDOM PLACED PRISMATIC PRESSURE SENSITIVE DISKS

3/8" DIA.

1/2" DIA.

3/4" DIA.

1/4" CLEAR ACRYLIC

SLOT - 1/4" x 3/4"

SLOT - 1/4" x 1"

PLAN

68

Cut out the tree with a saber or coping saw.

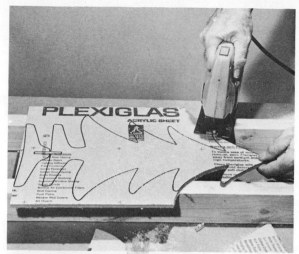

Use the back of a hacksaw blade ground or filed square to scrape the edges.

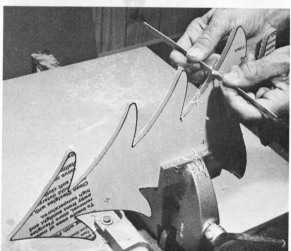

Polish the edges with a dampened cloth charged with auto polishing compound.

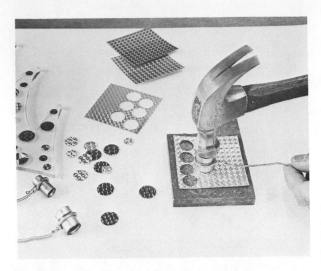

Clicker punches held with wire neatly cut the disks. Hardboard backup block should be used.

ÉTAGÈRE.   This handsome étagère is made with 18 equal-size pieces of transparent blue ¼" acrylic sheet and four strips of redwood.

The acrylic pieces are slightly under 4" × 18" to permit sawing all of them from a single 36" × 36" stock-size sheet. This allows for saw-kerf waste. If you prefer to cut the pieces by scribing, there will be no waste, thus they can be a full 4" × 18".

Cut the pieces to size, then scrape and sand the edges. Apply masking tape to cover the edges which will be cement-joined to guard against rounding, then proceed to buff and polish the rest of the edges.

Use thickened cement to make the side-by-side edge joints. Lay the three sections on a board with slots cut into it so the joint lines of the acrylic will line up over the gaps. The gaps will allow the squeezed-out cement to drop clear of the work. Apply a bead of cement to one edge of the joint, then bring the parts together. Two nails tacked along the outside edges will supply the necessary clamping pressure.

Cut four pieces of wood to size and cut ¼"-wide slots ¼" deep to receive the shelf units. If you have a table saw you can cut the slots with a dado cutter. Otherwise use a hand saw and chisel.

Quick-setting epoxy such as Devcon 5 Minute Epoxy is used to join the acrylic to the wood. Drill small depressions into both surfaces of the shelves in the areas which will be concealed by the wood. Do this by starting the point of a ¼" drill. These depressions will fill with epoxy in the joint, thus providing a more positive, locked grip.

Assembly begins by taping the two rear uprights to a flat work table. Apply epoxy sparingly to the grooves, working one shelf at a time. Check for plumb with a level.

The side uprights are next. This step necessitates fast, neat work, because the epoxy must be applied to six joints in rapid succession. Lay the third upright on the table, then position the assembly over it, propped with wood as shown in the photograph, so each shelf is in line and close to, but not touching, the slots in the upright. The exact location for the upright should be pre-marked on the plastic with a china marker during a dry test assembly.

Slide the upright slightly to one side to allow access to the grooves, then apply the epoxy. Work fast. Slide the upright into position, remove the prop stick at the front of the shelves, and allow them to drop into place in the grooves. Repeat the step for the last upright.

For safety in use the two rear uprights should be secured to the wall with appropriate fasteners.

Plastic and wood are combined in this unique étagère.

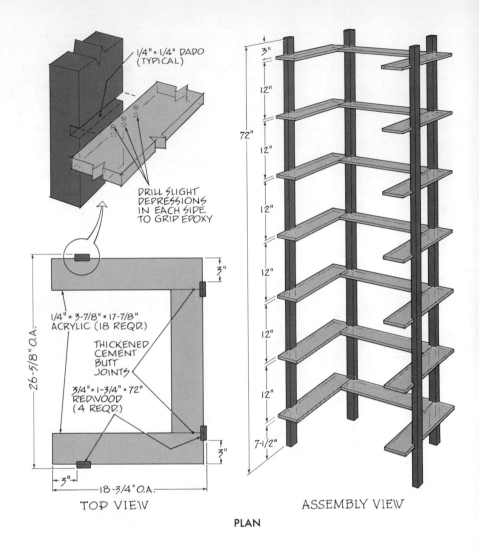

1/4" × 1/4" DADO (TYPICAL)

DRILL SLIGHT DEPRESSIONS IN EACH SIDE TO GRIP EPOXY

3"

1/4" × 3-7/8" × 17-7/8" ACRYLIC (18 REQD.)

THICKENED CEMENT BUTT JOINTS

3/4" × 1-3/4" × 72" REDWOOD (4 REQD.)

26-5/8" O.A.

3"

3"

3"

18-3/4" O.A.

TOP VIEW

3"

12"

12"

12"

72"

12"

12"

12"

7-1/2"

ASSEMBLY VIEW

PLAN

Shelf sections are ganged to save time in sanding. Sharp edges are later eased by sanding them individually.

ACRYLIC SHEET

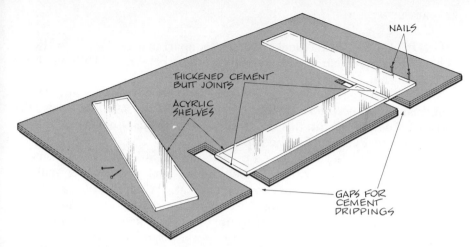

Use thickened cement to join the pieces. The setup shown will prevent the cement run-off from smearing the surfaces.

Attach the shelf sections to the back strips first. Check alignment with a square.

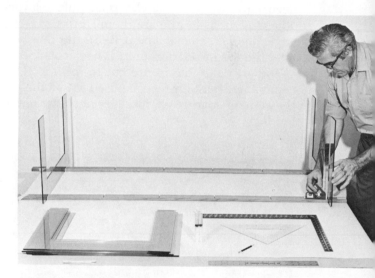

This phase of assembly is tricky. Use wood props to support the sections over the slots in the side strip. Remove the front prop when epoxy has been applied and slots are in position.

MONDRIAN TABLE.   Blocks of color set apart in a geometric gridwork of bold black lines characterize the works of the celebrated Dutch painter Piet Mondrian.

This interesting fold-down acrylic table features a top panel inspired by Mondrian's *Composition with Red, Blue and Yellow, 1930.* Whereas the artist worked with paint, this rendition utilizes brilliant color in the form of translucent Plexiglas for the top panel.

To make the table you'll need a piece of ½" × 30" × 30" clear acrylic. The art panel is made with ⅛" stock. Make the leg sections by cutting 20" into the square with the saw fence set at 3¼". If a table saw is not available you can use a saber saw. Next, make four radius cuts as indicated, then smooth all cut surfaces by scraping. After the legs are formed you can scrape the newly exposed edges. All edges are sanded to a satin finish.

A 250-watt infrared heat lamp can be used to form the legs. Place a block of wood with a 2" radius cut at one end under the part to be formed. Secure the work with a clamp and place layers of aluminum foil on the adjoining areas to insulate them from the heat. Apply heat until a right-angle bend is achieved (be patient, this takes time). Remove the heat and hold the leg in position until it has cooled.

The art panel pieces are cut to form a 21" × 21" square. Thickened cement and masking tape are used to join the pieces to the tabletop. Apply the cement sparingly, especially near the outer edges, to avoid squeeze-out.

Colored Plexiglas panels of this tabletop recreate geometric design of Mondrian painting. Drape-forming thick stock like this is a challenge, but it can be done with a heat lamp and patience.

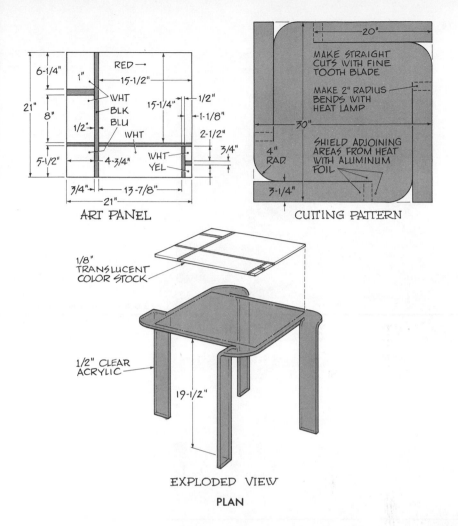

ART PANEL

6-1/4"
RED →
1"
15-1/2"
21"
WHT
BLK
BLU
15-1/4"
1/2"
1-1/8"
8"
1/2"
WHT
2-1/2"
3/4"
WHT
5-1/2"
4-3/4"
YEL
3/4"
13-7/8"
21"

CUTTING PATTERN

20"

MAKE STRAIGHT
CUTS WITH FINE
TOOTH BLADE

MAKE 2" RADIUS
BENDS WITH
HEAT LAMP

30"

4"
RAD

SHIELD ADJOINING
AREAS FROM HEAT
WITH ALUMINUM
FOIL

3-1/4"

1/8"
TRANSLUCENT
COLOR STOCK

1/2" CLEAR
ACRYLIC

19-1/2"

EXPLODED VIEW

PLAN

Four partial cuts are made
into the square panel before
forming the legs.

Block of wood with end cut on a 2" radius is clamped in place for forming.

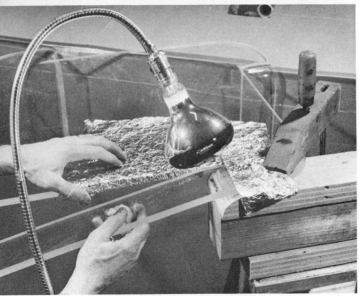

Aluminum foil is used to shield adjoining areas from heat. When the plastic begins to bend, guide it with the hand so it forms squarely, but *don't* force it down. It must drape voluntarily.

SEE-THROUGH COFFEE TABLE. The parts for this table are cut from a single sheet of clear acrylic ¼" × 36" × 36".

A table saw is ideal for the straight cutting, but a saber saw or portable circular saw can also be used if you guide it carefully. You can also make the cuts by the scribing-and-breaking method, but you will still need a coping saw for cutting the curved corner pieces.

To cut by scribing, clamp a straightedge to the sheet and make seven or eight passes with the scriber. Place the scribed line, face up, over a dowel and apply downward pressure to make the break.

Scrape all edges to remove tool marks, then sand to a satin finish, making certain the edges which are to be cemented are made perfectly flat. Those edges which will not be cemented can be further fine-finished by sanding and buffing to a transparent high gloss before assembly, or you can do this after final assembly.

Assemble the table in two stages. First assemble the four sides as individual units, and then cement them to each other and to the top in one final assembly. Use thickened cement to join two legs to each cross member, following the procedure described for the preceding Etagère project. The corner sections can be added later, also with thickened cement.

When the four leg sections are completed, tape them together with the corners butted. Secure the rectangular unit to the top with tape and apply cement. Solvent cement works best when the joints are in a horizontal position, so the table will have to be repositioned accordingly for each application.

A final buffing over joint lines and a wash with soap and water will bring out the sparkle.

See-through coffee table can be built with a minimal amount of material. Parts are cut from one sheet of 36″ × 36″ acrylic.

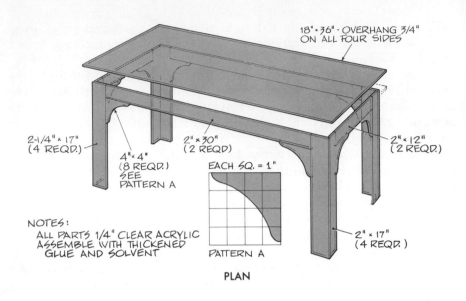

18" × 36" - OVERHANG 3/4" ON ALL FOUR SIDES

2-1/4" × 17"
(4 REQD.)

4" × 4"
(8 REQD.)
SEE
PATTERN A

2" × 30"
(2 REQD)

2" × 12"
(2 REQD.)

EACH SQ. = 1"

NOTES:
ALL PARTS 1/4" CLEAR ACRYLIC
ASSEMBLE WITH THICKENED
GLUE AND SOLVENT

PATTERN A

2" × 17"
(4 REQD.)

PLAN

Cutting the corner pieces. The curved section can also be cut with a coping saw.

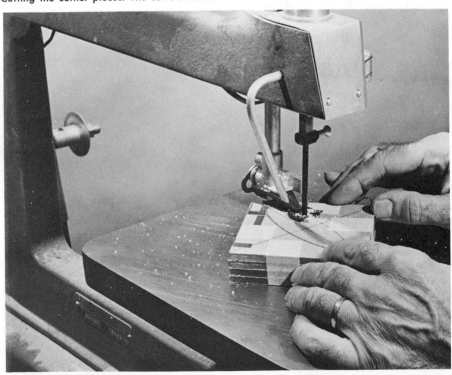

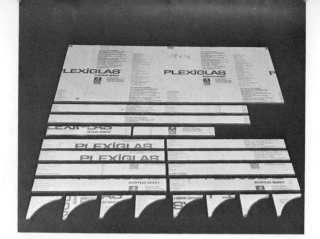

All the parts ready for edge finishing. Buff-polish only those edges which will not be cement-joined.

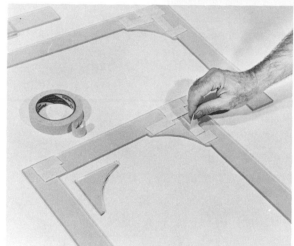

Tape the leg subassemblies together to check the fit of the parts, then disassemble and join the leg assemblies only with thickened cement in the manner described for the étagère. Solvent cement is used for final assembly.

Tape the leg assemblies to the top and butt them at the corners. Apply solvent cement. Note how the piece is propped with stick to keep it level so the solvent doesn't run downhill and off the end.

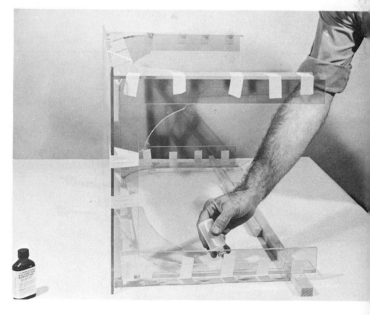

ACRYLIC GLAZING.   Storm windows and shower doors, or glazed constructions of any type, are easily fabricated with acrylic glazing ($\frac{1}{10}''$ thickness) in combination with Reynolds Do-It-Yourself aluminum storm sash sections and corner-lock fittings, which are commonly available at hardware and building-supply dealers.

The project shown here—a miniature greenhouse—illustrates the potential for out-of-the-ordinary usage of these materials, but the same technique is used for making any doors or windows. Proceed as follows.

Measure the height and width of the opening to determine the outside dimension of the frame. Mark two lengths (minus $\frac{1}{8}''$) of storm sash sections for the side members and two widths (minus $\frac{1}{8}''$) for the top and bottom. Remove the rubber glazing channels from these pieces.

Mark 45° angles at the measured points and saw off the ends, using a hacksaw. Smooth the ends by filing or sanding.

Scribe-cut acrylic glazing $1\frac{1}{16}''$ less than the outside frame size, in both

Acrylic glazing is far superior to glass in terms of durability and ease of fabrication.

directions. Scrape or file a slight bevel around each edge to break sharp corners before removing the protective masking.

Insert the glazing channel over the plastic and use a razor blade to trim mitered ends. Press the sash channel into place over the rubber. If you have trouble with the fit, wet the groove in the aluminum channel with a solution of one part water to one part dish detergent.

Insert corner locks into the top and bottom sections, then slide them into the side frame members to complete the assembly. Note that the corner-lock fittings are for right-angle applications only, but they can easily be adapted for use at the point of a triangle. For this you use tin snips to cut away a wedge out of the center portion. This will allow the fitting to bend to a sharper angle.

Scribing and breaking is the best way to cut large sheets to size.

Rubber glazing channel is removed from the aluminum storm sash sections and inserted over the edge of the glazing.

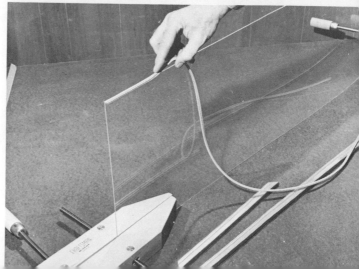

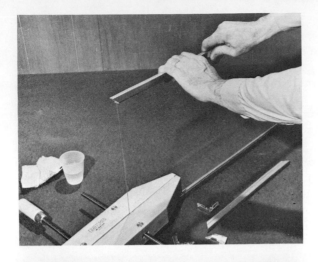

Use water and detergent to lubricate the channel, then press into place.

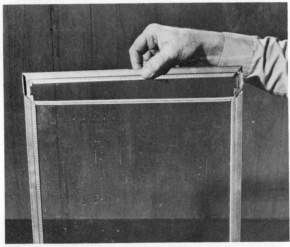

Corner-lock fittings effectively hold the mitered corners in place.

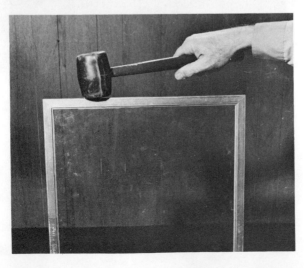

A few light taps with a sott mallet snug the fit.

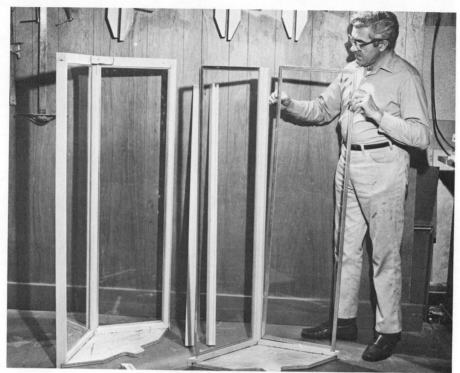

The made-up sections are substantial enough to use freestanding, but they're inserted into special framing for this particular application.

The corner locks can be adapted for unusual usage such as this.

11 | Casting Liquid Plastic

There is another way to make things of plastic without the use of tools—by casting liquid plastic in a mold. Upon solidifying the plastic is removed from the mold, revealing a perfect duplication of the shape of the mold in opposite form.

Numerous casting materials are available, but polyester resin is the kind most widely used for hobby work. This is a clear liquid with the consistency of maple syrup. A second liquid, the catalyst or "hardener," is added to the resin in very small prescribed amounts prior to pouring. This sets up a chemical reaction that solidifies the resin.

The materials are available at handicrafts and hobby-supply shops as well as at some of the acrylics distributors. In addition to the resin and hardener you can also obtain a wide variety of plastic molds, transparent and opaque dyes, and embedding materials.

The molds and embedding materials are relatively inexpensive, but you can use a variety of ordinary household items for the molds as well as for the embedment specimens. Drinking glasses, ash trays, food storage containers, tin and aluminum cans, or practically any smooth-surfaced, non-porous containers or objects that have the desired shape can be used for molds. Embedments may be trinkets, coins, stamps, dried flowers and leaves, even photographs, to name a few.

If the object you select for a mold has tapered sides with an opening larger than the bottom, the casting usually can be released and the intact mold used again. However, if the mold is undercut with a projection, it will have to be broken or cut apart in order to free the casting. If salvage of the mold is important to you, check the mold carefully in advance to make sure that even the most minute undercut is not present.

Flexible or semirigid molds can be flexed to release the casting. Rigid molds such as tin or aluminum cans can be cut apart with snips. Rigid molds such as glassware can be coated with mold release agent to simplify removal of the casting. This usually can be obtained in a spray can where you buy the resin.

Three examples of poured plastic projects. Owl plaque
(top) and coaster (above) are made with plastic molds
purchased in a craft shop. Drinking glass served as mold
for flower embedment (right).

HARDENER. Casting is a relatively simple operation. However, the addition of the proper amount of hardener to the resin is very important. Contrary to what you might naturally assume, large castings require proportionately less hardener than small ones. It depends upon the thickness of the piece to be cast rather than on volume. For example, 8 ounces of resin poured into a ½"-thick mold may require 16 drops of hardener whereas the same amount of resin poured into a cup may require only 6 drops. It's a matter of heat—the chemical reaction that occurs during solidifying generates heat. A broad surface dissipates heat more readily than a thick mass. Too much hardener in a thick section builds up more heat than it can handle, thus resulting in a cracked casting.

Specific hardener/resin ratios are not recommended here because they vary between brands. Each manufacturer provides tables giving the proper ratios for various-size castings. They should be followed with care.

The curing or hardening occurs in two stages. The resin first gels, developing a rubbery consistency somewhat like dessert gelatin, then it becomes progressively harder, usually reaching the solid state in a matter of hours or overnight (depending upon variables such as room temperature, humidity, and the amount of hardener used). The full cure develops in about a week. The casting can be removed from the mold upon hardening.

POURING. When the mold is ready, pour the required amount of resin into a disposable container such as an empty food jar or a paper cup (cleaning the container for reuse is too difficult). The catalyst or hardener usually comes in a tube or squeeze bottle which dispenses one drop at a time. Consult the manufacturer's chart, then add the prescribed amount of hardener to the resin. Stir the hardener into the resin thoroughly for about a minute. If you want to obtain a colored casting, add and mix in the colorant before adding the hardener. If the mixture is pocked with bubbles, let it stand for about a minute until they clear. Some air bubbles may develop in the casting, but they usually float up to the top and break free.

Once the hardener has been added, the reaction begins, so don't delay the pouring for any extended time. Should the mix begin to gel during the pour, you will have to discard it and begin the process again with a new batch of resin in a cleaned-out mold. Acetone is used to remove resin before it hardens; detergent to clean the hands. Work in a well-ventilated room, and don't get the chemicals in the eyes or mouth.

EMBEDDING. This is simply a process of enclosing objects in plastic. This may be done in a single pour or in two or more, depending upon the effect desired. If the object can be suspended from the outside of the mold, a single pour will suffice. When the object is to be fully surrounded by plastic, a partial first pour is necessary. This forms a base for the embedment to rest upon, after which a subsequent pour is made.

In order to obtain a clear casting without a demarcation between layers, the additional layer must be poured while the first stage is in the gel state. If you want to suspend more than one object at different levels throughout the casting, you simply make multiple pours. Less hardener is used for the in-between pours, since the previous pours build up heat. The final pour gets the same amount of hardener as the first one.

PROJECTS.   Examples of three basic types of casting are illustrated; all are easy and fun to do.

Owl plaque.   This wall plaque is made with a ready-made plastic mold. You color it with opaque pigments which are mixed with a small amount of resin and hardener. Apply the pigment mixture to the inside surface of the mold before the main pour of resin. Allow each of the varied colors to gel before applying the subsequent one in order to keep them from bleeding into each other. When the eyes, beak, feet, and overall feather highlights have been colored, prepare the main pour. This is also colored to a brown mix for overall background, then poured to fill the mold.

Polyester resin is air-inhibited—that is, it remains tacky on the part which is exposed to air. After the resin has hardened, put a piece of freezer wrap over the tacky surface to exclude air, permitting it to harden.

The oval plaque is made with a piece of ½" plywood. Use epoxy to attach the casting to the wood. Refer to Chapter 3 on measuring and marking for details on drawing an oval.

First step in casting the owl plaque shown on page 85. Opaque colors are mixed with resin and hardener and applied to bottom of mold.

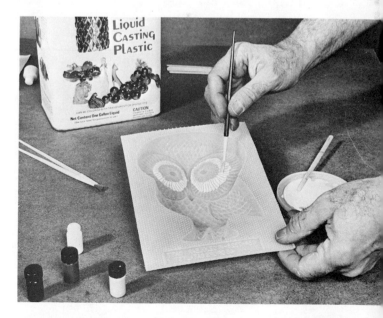

Pigment color is added to resin and thoroughly mixed before adding hardener.

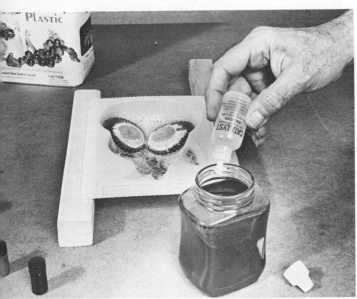

Catalyst hardener is added to colored resin and mixed thoroughly for one minute.

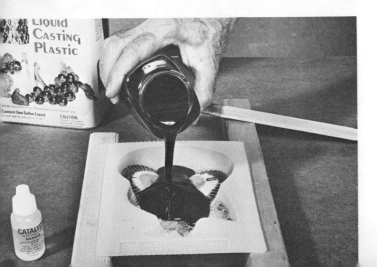

Final pour is added while painted areas are still in a state of gel.

Fern is placed on tacky first pour. Mold is then filled with resin to the top.

Coaster. The coaster is also cast in a ready-made mold (American Handicrafts Co.). This mold has "two-up" so that you can make two coasters at one time. Dehydrated fern is the embedment, available from the same supplier as well as most handicrafts shops.

In order to suspend the fern, make the pour in two stages. Pour the first layer to cover the entire bottom surface only. When the resin gels, place the leaves carefully on the tacky surface. Then follow with the final pour.

Flower embedment. Two flower embedments are shown. The short paperweight is made with realistic but artificial flowers. The other one is made with dried natural flowers obtained at a floral-supply shop. Both are made with single pours in drinking-glass molds. The stems which project from the bottom of the mold permit easy suspension of the specimens with spring clips. When suspending any object it is important to position it so it doesn't touch the outside of the mold so it will be surrounded by resin.

When you remove the casting from the mold, trim the stems flush and sand the bottom (after a one-week cure). The tall casting was easily removed from the glass by inserting a knife point around the lip to loosen it. The short casting would not release from the glass because of the slight inward bulge near the top, which locked it in. A series of longitudinal scores made with a glass cutter were made around the glass. This was then placed in a strong paper bag and struck on the thick part of the glass with a hammer to break it free. Wear work gloves for extra protection when doing this, and remove glass splinters remaining on the casting by washing with running water.

Spring clothespins hold the embedment in suspension.

Colorful paperweight is made with artificial crocus flowers.

Squeeze bottle dispenses one drop of hardener at a time.

Making the single pour.

Glass cutter is used to weaken the tumbler so it breaks easily.

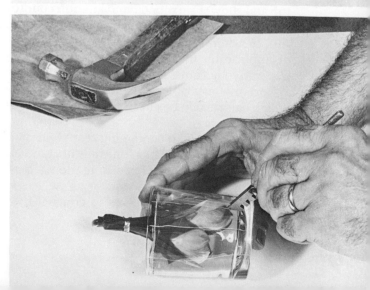

12 | Man-made Marble

Corian sheet is an intriguing, relatively new member of the family of plastics. You may have seen it and perhaps even touched the material and mistakenly assumed it to be marble. This is understandable, since the product is a remarkable marble look-alike. It has the elegance of fine marble, with subtle coloring, delicate veining, and a rich opalescence. But there the similarity ends.

Corian sheet has properties which render it superior to the real thing in terms of strength, durability, ease of maintenance, and, not the least among its outstanding features, workability. Consequently, the material is ideally suited for do-it-yourself applications.

Corian is a cast material of filled methyl methacrylate polymer manufactured by DuPont. Although it is closely related chemically to the acrylics covered in the previous chapters of this book, it differs physically in appearance as well as in two aspects of fabrication: It cannot be solvent-cemented, nor can it be heat-formed.

Corian was developed primarily as an improved material for vanity tops, tub and shower surrounds, and kitchen countertops. Other typical applications include wall panels, wainscots, baseboards, thresholds, and window-sills. In addition, imaginative home craftsmen have broadened the scope of application by utilizing it as a craft material with which to create decorative accents and furnishings, with impressive results.

Corian is available in dimension sheets of ¼", ½", and ¾" thickness which can readily be cut to size for custom installations and general fabrication purposes.

A bathtub wall kit containing ready-cut panels and a center batten strip is available for installation on walls in standard 5-foot tub enclosures. The panels can be placed over existing tile walls as well as over dry wall. A tub wall trim kit is also obtainable for use where Corian sheet is installed over existing tile. The trim serves to conceal the gap between the wall and sheet at the edges.

Corian sheet looks and feels very much like real marble.

Sheet stock cut to dimension is used for nonstandard-size tub enclosures or for shower surrounds and for customizing countertops.

The most luxurious way to go for remodeling or new construction of kitchen countertops or bathroom vanities is to use one-piece tops which have integrally molded sinks. The precast construction eliminates joints and makes installation quite easy, since no cutouts are necessary. Installation simply involves the application of a few dabs of adhesive to the top

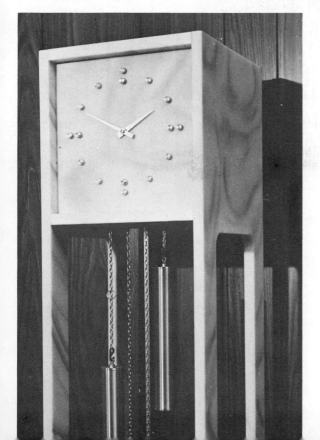

Corian is well suited to craft projects, as it can be cut and drilled with ordinary tools.

edges of the support. The backsplash which is provided is also attached with adhesive.

As you can see in the accompanying list, vanity tops come in a wide range of sizes, shapes, colors and bowl positions. Kitchen countertops are available with either a single or double sink. A wet-bar top comes with an offset bowl and no predrilled faucet holes to allow a choice of left-end or right-end sink positions.

Corian is readily available through a nationwide network of dealers, fabricators, and installers. They can be found in the Yellow Pages under "Corian Building Products by DuPont" in the general listing of "Kitchen Cabinets and Equipment."

Cost varies with thickness, width, and color. While the initial cost may

---

Summary of Standard CORIAN® Products

Corian Sheet Standard Sizes	Thickness		
	¼″	½″	¾″
30″×57″	X		
30″×72″	X		
30″×98″	X	X	X
22″+8″×98″		X	
25″+5″×98″		X	X
25″×98″		X	X
30″×121″		X	X
22″+8″×121″		X	X
25″+5″×121″		X	X
25″×121″		X	X
30″×145″		X	X

Bathtub Wall Kit
    4 pieces ¼″×29⁵/₁₆″×57″
    1 piece ¼″×6″×57″

Bath Trim Kits
    ½″ 4 pieces 2″×74″
    ¾″ 4 pieces 2″×74″

Countertop Trim
    ¼″×1″×57″
    ¼″×1″×98″

Accessories
    Scotch Brite® wiping pads
    Silicone Sealant
    Hardware for Mounting Bowls
    Adhesive and Caulk
    Heat Conductive Tape

Standard Patterns & Colors

Cameo White—opalescent white, no pattern.

Dawn Beige & Olive Mist—with delicate veining all the way through.

Autumn Gold—subtle, dappled-yellow pattern all the way through. Only available in ½″ or ¾″ sheet.

be higher than that of ordinary materials, Corian is less expensive in the long run due to its lasting qualities.

Corian is not recommended for structural, flooring, or below-grade applications. Designs where moisture could be trapped behind the material without ventilation such as damp walls must be avoided.

The material can withstand a reasonable degree of high temperature and normal countertop abuse, but hot pans should not be placed directly on the surface, nor should it be used as a cutting board.

Corian has good resistance to a wide range of chemicals, but some groups of chemicals can stain or etch the surface. These include strong acids (such as concentrated sulfuric acid), ketones (like acetone), chlorinated solvents (like chloroform), or strong solvent combinations like paint

Corian Integrally Molded Tops & Bowls

Sizes	Bowl Position*	Sizes	Bowl Position*
Vanity Single Bowl		22" × 102"	24"-LCR-24"
17" × 19"	C	**Vanity Double Bowl**	
17" × 21"	C	22" × 49"	12½"-LR-12½"
17" × 25"	C	22" × 61"	15½"-LR-15½"
19½" × 25"	C	22" × 73"	18½"-LR-18½"
19½" × 31"	C	22" × 85"	18½"-LR-18½"
19½" × 37"	C	22" × 102"	27"-LR-27"
22" × 25"	C	**Vanity Banjo Style**	
22" × 31"	C	22" × 61"	12½"-LR-12½"
22" × 37"	C	**Vanity Corner Bowl**	No Backsplash
22" × 43"	C	25"	C
22" × 49"	15"-LCR-15"	**Bar Top & Sink**	No Faucet Holes
22" × 61"	15"-LCR-15"	22" × 61"	15" Reversible
22" × 67"	15"-LCR-15"	25" × 61"	No Faucet Holes
22" × 73"	18"-LCR-18"		15" Reversible
22" × 85"	18"-LCR-18"	**Kitchen Top & Sink**	Std. 8" Faucet Holes
		25" × 121"	(3) C

*C-Center, L-Left, R-Right. For non-centered bowls, bowl positions are shown in inches from edge of top to center of drain. Vanity tops and bowls supplied with standard 4" faucet holes unless otherwise specified.

Make sure you specify color, length, width, thickness, bowl position, and faucet holes (if other than standard).

remover. With the exception of paint remover, short periods of contact will usually not cause serious damage.

Use of ¼" sheet should generally be restricted to vertical applications; it is not recommended for use as a countertop. The choice between ½" and ¾" for a particular application is generally a matter of aesthetics, unless impact resistance or the allowable overhang is a design consideration. The maximum unsupported and unloaded overhang is 12" for ¾" sheet and 6" for ½" sheet.

The recommended expansion clearance for uncaulked joints is ¹⁄₃₂" for every 8' in length. Joints which are to be caulked should be ¹⁄₁₆" to ⅛" wide to allow for satisfactory caulking penetration.

Corian building products are compatible with most commercially available caulking sealants, but silicone sealant is the type most highly recommended. DuPont distributors offer a translucent white silicone that blends well with the background color of Corian sheet and enhances the appearance of the finished job.

Corian is made with a nonrepeating pattern to avoid an artificial appearance. Thus, like natural materials, panels may vary slightly in coloration and pattern intensity. For the most pleasing installation, panels that are compatible should be selected before starting fabrication.

The preceding general specifications and the following installation photographs and illustrations are copyrighted by and supplied through the courtesy of E. I. du Pont de Nemours & Company, Corian® Building Products.

This bathroom features a Corian vanity and tub surround.

This one-piece molded kitchen sink is complemented by a custom-fabricated countertop.

A bar top with integrally cast sink is available for entertainment-center renovations.

13 | Working with Corian

Corian sheet can be machined with conventional woodworking tools—it responds much like dense hardwood. Actually, being a member of the acrylic family of plastics, it can be machined in essentially the same manner as "conventional" acrylic plastic. With minor exceptions, the procedures described for working with acrylics apply to Corian. This material is considerably tougher than thermoplastic acrylic, however, and therefore it is somewhat slower-cutting.

Sheet stock has a face or "good" side; the back is not smooth-polished. The face side is protected with a peel-off film of clear plastic, which is left on during general handling but removed for layout marking and machining.

SAWING.   Straight cuts are best made using a stationary saw with a carbide-tipped blade. Conventional blades can also be used but will dull rapidly. In any case, the greater the number of teeth, the smoother the resulting cut. Large-tooth, deep-set ripsaw blades are not recommended.

Chipping does occur to a minor degree along the bottom of the kerf, so the material should be cut with the face side up when using any of the stationary saws. When sawing, feed the work slowly and be sure to provide off-table support for large workpieces.

Rabbets and dadoes can be cut with a regular sawblade or with a dado head. Don't try to make any groove of appreciable width and depth in one pass with a dado cutter because of the strain this would impart on the tool in addition to the possibility of a dangerous kickback. Make several passes instead, to achieve the desired full depth of cut. If a dado cutter is not available, the repeat-kerf method will prove quite satisfactory.

Rabbet cuts are frequently required, particularly for making trim strips to finish off a Corian tub or shower surround installation over ceramic tile and for edge treatments on table or countertops. When using a sawblade in lieu of a dado cutter, make the first cut into the edge of the stock and the second cut on the flat surface. If the rabbet edge is faced inboard (against the fence), be sure to stand off to the side, out of the blade line. When the waste piece is cut free it may be kicked back like an arrow.

Because of the excessive weight of a large sheet (a ¾" × 30" × 121" piece weighs about 175 pounds), you will find it much easier to move a saw over the work rather than to move the work over a stationary saw. The portable circular saw is therefore indispensable for cutting large sheets to working size. When using this saw, place the Corian sheet face up on sawhorses and 2 × 4 lumber support rails. Masking tape applied to the surface will prevent tool scratches. Clamp a straightedge to the sheet to guide the saw and adjust the depth of cut so the blade protrudes from the sheet about ¼". Always position the support rails so the work and cutoff won't sag at the end of the cut.

The band saw, jigsaw, and saber saw can be used for making straight and curved cuts when equipped with metal-cutting blades. Since the saber saw cuts on the upstroke, any chipping that may occur will be on the surface facing up. If the cut edge will subsequently be exposed to view, the sheet should be cut with the good face down. A blade with 14 teeth per inch works well with the saber saw. A tungsten carbide "toothless" grit blade can be used in the saber saw; it will last a long time, but does cut rather slowly.

Inside cutouts are made with the saber saw after drilling a blade-entry hole. Concealed openings for plumbing fixtures and accessories can be cut freehand, but finish cuts are made with a clamped-on saw guide. As was discussed with acrylics, sharp inside corners result in stress concentrations which could develop into cracks, so you should avoid them. Use a ⅜" minimum diameter drill to form the corner radii before sawing.

MAKING HOLES.   Good clean holes can be made in Corian sheet with twist drills, flat spade bits, fly cutters, and hole saws. Moderate woodworking speeds are recommended for all but the fly cutter. Always use a backup block to prevent edge chipping when drilling through holes.

Deep holes with twist drills usually necessitate frequent retraction for cooling and to prevent clogging of the flutes. Spade bits, on the other hand, are fed continuously to achieve smooth-edged walls. The filmy large shavings produced by this tool readily emerge from the hole without clogging, provided the tool is sharp. Small workpieces in particular should be clamped for this operation.

Hole saws are useful for making through holes for plumbing. They usually produce a slightly rough-edged wall, which is of no consequence for this purpose. When you use a hole saw in a drill press, however, you can achieve a somewhat smoother edge by increasing the rpm while decreasing the feed rate.

Large holes beyond the capacity of hole saws or drill bits can be made with a fly cutter in the drill press. Clamp the work firmly and use the lowest rpm. Increase the speed only if stalling occurs when moderate feed pressure is applied.

ROUTING. The router is useful for a variety of fabrication operations. It may be used for cutting rabbets and dadoes, forming decorative molded edges, and making internal cutouts. Carbide cutters are essential for good results. Piloted cutters for decorative edges should be of the ball-bearing type in order to avoid friction overheating problems. When deep cuts are required, it is advisable to make repeat passes, perhaps two or three, until you reach full depth.

An edge which is to be routed with a piloted cutter must be smooth and free of saw ripples or other irregularities, because the finished cut will exactly duplicate that edge. Rabbet cuts and molded edges are made by simply riding the pilot against the edge, moving the tool from left to right.

A template guide in the router base used in conjunction with a template is used to make straight or irregular internal cutouts. Templates can be made of plywood or hardboard. An accessory pivot guide is used to make precise circular cuts. In general the router is moved in a clockwise direction for internal cuts.

SANDING. Corian building products respond well to open-coat aluminum oxide abrasive for general smoothing and stock removal. You can achieve a superb satin final finish with wet-or-dry silicone carbide paper.

A minimal amount of sanding will normally be required in tub and shower wall installations, because smooth "factory" edges are usually the only ones exposed to view. Therefore the extent of finish sanding in these applications usually will merely involve hand sanding with a block to ease sharp corners. This is done with 120 and then 220 grit paper.

In situations where an edge of a sheet requires stock removal in order to conform to an irregular or out-of-plumb wall, sawing may not be feasible if the amount to be trimmed off is too small to gain purchase with the blade. A portable belt sander with 80 grit abrasive will prove most effective for the task.

Tool marks on straight and outside curved edges are best removed with a finishing sander. Deep marks may require the use of 80 grit paper followed with 120 and 220. Hand sanding will progress more rapidly if several intermediate grades are used in the process. The stationary disc sander is useful for squaring edges and rounding corners on small workpieces.

When desired, craft projects can be fine-finished with wet-or-dry paper lubricated with water. Work with a padded block, starting with 220 grit and working up through 400. It is rarely necessary, but if you want a still-higher polish you can get it by buffing with a product such as DuPont White Auto Polishing Compound.

ADHESIVES.   Corian building products may be installed over conventional substrates such as water-resistant gypsum wallboard, plaster, plywood, and ceramic tile with neoprene-based panel adhesive. This adhesive is readily available in cartridge form for application with a caulking gun. The usual procedure for wall installations is to apply a continuous ¼″ bead to the wall near all edges, and vertically about 8″ apart. The sheet is pressed firmly against the wall, then pulled away to "string" the adhesive and to allow it to vent for about two minutes. The panel is then pressed back against the wall. Apply pressure with the palm of the hand or with a softwood block and mallet to ensure good contact.

For surfaces which require a moisture seal, such as standard gypsum wallboard, a solvent base spread mastic system is used. These mastics are also suitable for use as a leveling coat to smooth minor surface irregularities. This method is also recommended for installation over surfaces with highly contrasting colors, such as multicolored tile.

The spread mastic system is a two-step operation. Using a flat trowel, apply a thin smooth coat of adhesive to the entire surface of the wall much like a coat of heavy paint. This is the sealer coat. Allow it to dry for about one hour. Next, apply gobs of the same mastic to the wall and spread it with a V-notched trowel. The mastic adhesive has a working time of about 20 to 30 minutes; therefore the installation should be sequenced in stages to make certain the panels are installed before the adhesive films over.

Corian sheet may be joined to itself with Weld-On #16 Thickened Cement (available at acrylics-supply outlets) or with epoxy as well as with panel adhesive. When using any of these adhesives, avoid heavy clamp pressure. Moderate spring-clamp pressure or masking tape will serve to hold the parts in contact while the adhesive sets. It is important to avoid starving the joint by squeezing too much adhesive out of it.

Though the manufacturer advises against using ¼″ stock by itself for countertops, you can nevertheless use it for light-duty tabletops by laminating it to a solid support, such as a sheet of ¾″ plywood, for improved structural integrity. Panel adhesive is used to laminate the pieces in the same manner as described for wall installation.

MECHANICAL FASTENERS.   Threads may be cut in Corian sheet to permit fastening with screws, a necessary expedient for some craft projects. As with conventional acrylics, only NC threading forms should be used—fine threads are prone to apex fracture. Refer to the section on cutting threads in Chapter 5 for recommended procedures as well as tap and drill sizes.

14 | Installing a Corian Countertop

The following step-by-step procedure is intended as a guide for the installation of a simple L slab top in a remodeling job on existing kitchen cabinets.

Basic design. Planning is the first step. Start by making a simple top-view drawing of the countertop in the form of an L with overall dimensions indicated. Plan on using a butt rather than a mitered joint to form the L. Mitered joints should be avoided as they are difficult to make and wasteful of material. Refer to the stock size list to determine what size sheets will be most economical. The butt joint should be at least 3″ away from cooktop, sink, or other cutouts. This may dictate whether the joint line will run lengthwise or crosswise. Indicate the joint position on the drawing, then fill in the dimension for each slab.

A 5″ backsplash is standard and can be cut from a stock 30″-wide sheet. Add the splash pieces to the drawing with lengths indicated.

The usual procedure with Corian installations is to build up the cabinet top with 1″ × 2″ wood strips to raise the countertop height to accommodate appliances. The exposed edges of the build-up strips are later concealed with ¼″ × 1″ strips of Corian. Enter the dimensions of the strips to finalize the drawing.

Referring to the drawing, make up a "bill of materials" for ordering standard sizes of sheet material. Include neoprene panel adhesive, silicone sealant, and heat-conductive tape, as required.

Sample Bill of Materials

Description	Quantity	Size	Color	Use
Corian® Sheet	2	¾″×30″×121″	Dawn Beige	Countertop and splash
Corian® Sheet	3	¼″×1″×98″	Dawn Beige	Edge trim
Conductive Tape	1	2″ wide roll	(Aluminum Metal)	Cooktop cutout
Panel Adhesive	3	11 oz. caulk tubes	Tan	Glue top to cabinets
Silicone Sealant	1	1/12 gal. caulk tube	Translucent White	Caulk joints

Countertop of Corian is handsome and durable.

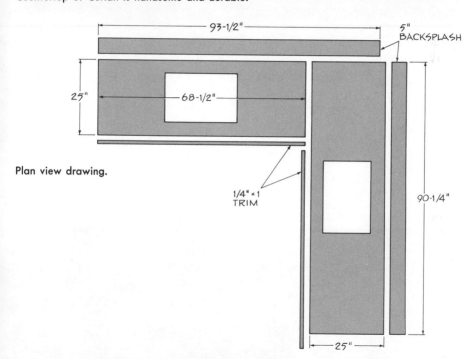

93-1/2"

5"
BACKSPLASH

25"

68-1/2"

Plan view drawing.

1/4" × 1
TRIM

90-1/4"

25"

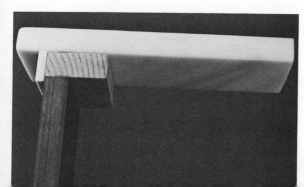

Typical build-up strip and
front-edge treatment.

Tools. The tools and supplies listed below include a full complement. Some are optional, depending upon your choice of fabrication methods.

Circular saw

Saber saw

Electric drill, ⅜″ bit

Router, ⅜″ carbide straight cutter

Decorative edge carbide router cutter

Router template

Belt sander

Finishing sander

Tape measure, square, level

Hammer, nails

Caulking gun

Putty knife

Sawhorses, 2 × 4 support rails

3′ and 8′ straightedges

Masking tape

Denatured alcohol

Cabinet tops framed with built-up stripping.

Preparation. It is advisable to do as much cutting as possible outdoors to minimize dust problems. Plastic dropcloths should be placed over doors and air ducts for dust control when indoor cutting is done.

Shut off gas, electrical, and water services and remove the old countertop. Install 1″ × 2″ wood build-up strips to the top of the cabinet framing. Check with a level and shim where necessary to obtain a true flat surface. A 1″ × 4″ flat board should be centered and nailed at the joint location to bridge the two Corian sheets. If any rear areas along the walls are without support, add cleats flush with the build-up strips. The strips along the exposed edges should be flush with the cabinet front to permit installation of the trim strips.

Countertop fabrication. Remove the protective film from the face of the sheet, then place the sheet face up on sawhorses bridged with 2 × 4 support rails. Refer to your drawing and mark the sheets for cutting. Allow a minimum ⅛″ clearance at return walls for expansion.

Adjust the support rails so the cutoff will not sag and break at the end of the cut. Set the blade for minimum projection, then clamp a straightedge in place to guide the saw. Make a rip cut from the 30″-wide sheet to obtain the 5″ backsplash. Next, cut the panel to length, arranging the cut so the joint between sheets will butt good factory edges together. Always wear safety glasses when sawing (or routing).

When the pieces have been cut, make a trial fit. If necessary, use the belt sander or notch out the wallboard to obtain a good fit. While the sheets are in place, mark them for the cutouts. Allow ¼″ minimum clearance between Corian and the appliance on all sides. Carry the work back to the sawhorses to make the cutouts.

Use a straightedge guide to rip the backsplash strip.

The cutout should be made with a router. Routing is done with the face side up, using a ⅜" straight cutter with a template guide inserted in the base of the router. Clamp a straightedge template in place and make only a partial cutout. Cut along the front and back edges and slightly around the corners. The remaining uncut material will provide strength during handling while the work is moved into the kitchen for final cutting. With help, carry the sheet on edge to the kitchen and place it on the cabinets.

Insert two thin slats under the cutout area to support the dropout piece, then proceed to finish the cutout, guiding the router with a clamped straightedge. When the cutout is complete, the strength of the sheet is considerably reduced in the narrow sections (until the countertop is secured with adhesive), so it must be handled with care. Ease all exposed edges by sanding.

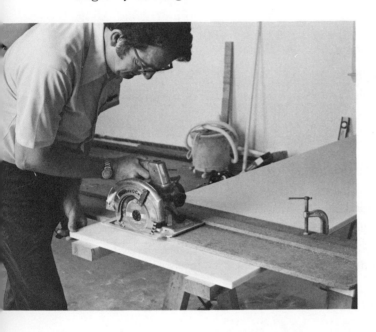

Cut the top to length. Good side should be face down when using a portable circular saw.

Allow ¼" clearance for cooktop cutout.

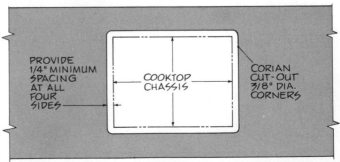

PROVIDE 1/4" MINIMUM SPACING AT ALL FOUR SIDES

COOKTOP CHASSIS

CORIAN CUT-OUT 3/8" DIA. CORNERS

Use a template guide router accessory and a wood template to make the cutout.

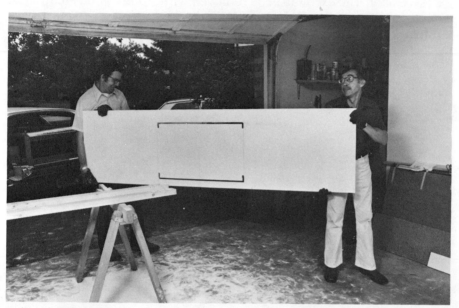

Make only a partial cutout if the workpiece is to be transported to the kitchen.

Use wood slats to support the waste when completing the cutout in place.

Countertop installation. The best way to obtain a good seal at the butt joint is to push one sheet toward the other to squeeze out excess sealant. Therefore it is important to decide which sheet to install first to permit this action.

Remove all dust and particles from the Corian sheet and the cabinet tops. Wipe the butt-joint surfaces with an alcohol-dampened cloth to assure good adhesion of the sealant.

Carefully tilt one Corian sheet up away from the cabinet top. Apply small dabs of neoprene adhesive at 12″ intervals all around the supports. Then lower the top into its final position. Repeat the procedure for the second sheet, but set it down about ½″ away from the first one.

Apply a continuous bead of silicone sealant to the joint between the two sheets. Then push the second sheet firmly against the other to squeeze out excess sealant. The excess may be removed with a putty knife followed by a cleanup with an alcohol-dampened cloth. Or the excess sealant may be left to harden for several hours; it can then be trimmed off with a razor blade.

Apply adhesive in small dabs on all the build-up strips.

Apply a full bead of silicone
sealant to joint.

Push the slab into the joint
to squeeze out excess sealant.

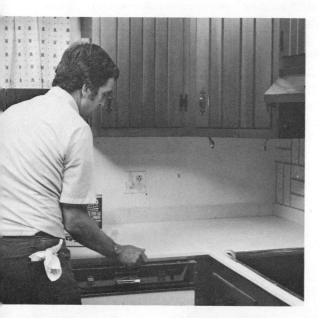

Excess sealant can be
trimmed with a razor blade
after it has set up for several
hours.

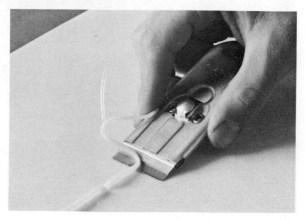

Appliance, trim, and backsplash installation.   The opening for a drop-in cooktop must be lined with pressure-sensitive aluminum conductive tape. This tape is 2″ wide and should be applied so it folds over on the top surface as far as the cooktop rim. The remaining tape is folded underneath the countertop. The cooktop is installed in the usual manner, centered in the opening, and the fasteners finger-tightened only enough to prevent movement.

A drop-in sink is installed in the same manner, but with the aluminum tape omitted. The rim of the sink may be bedded in silicone sealant or plumber's putty for a watertight seal.

The backsplash can now be installed. Measure and cut the splash to length, then sand all sharp edges and smooth the sawed edge to remove any saw ripples. The splash should be installed with the sawed edge down, the factory edge up. Apply a continuous bead of silicone sealant along the rear edge of the countertop and small dabs every 6″ on the wall area behind the splash. Set the splash into position and brace it, if necessary, to assure a good fit. Quickly remove the excess sealant with a putty knife and wipe clean with alcohol.

The ¼″ × 1″ edge trim is installed directly on the cabinet front under the countertop overhang with dabs of panel adhesive. Secure the strips in place with masking tape or with fine nails propped against the edges until the adhesive has set.

Apply conductive tape around cooktop opening.

Masking tape holds edge trim while adhesive sets up.

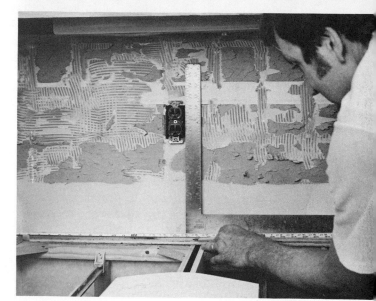

Make careful measurements for cutouts when installing a full-height backsplash.

Customizing options

Backsplash. The use of a standard 5″ backsplash is not a hard-and-fast rule. If desired, a 3″ backsplash could be used. The leftover 2″ strip may then be utilized for front-edge treatments.

A full-height backsplash covering the entire wall between the counter-top and wall cabinets is another possibility. For this you could use ¼″-thick Corian sheet installed directly on top of the countertop.

Measure all dimensions carefully and spot openings for outlets. Cut the sheet to size, using a saber or circular saw. Drill ⅜″ holes to form the corners for sawing the outlet openings and other inside corners. Adhere the splash to the wall with neoprene adhesive or silicone sealant. Seal the joint at the countertop in the same manner as a regular backsplash.

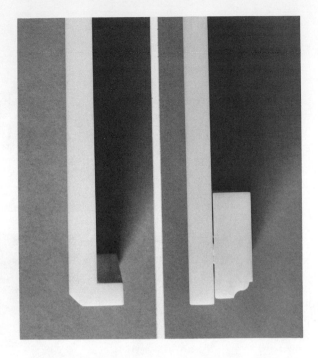

Edge-treatment options: drop
edge with chamfered edge
and shaped build-up strip.

Edge treatment. The countertop edge need not be plain. It can be routed with shaped cutters to create a sculptured effect. Use a carbide cutter with ball-bearing pilot for this.

The drop edge is another variation. Corian strips glued directly to the front edge of the countertop will give it a thick look. This is best done before the countertop is installed. Use Weld-On #16 Thickened Cement to attach the strip. Spread the cement liberally on the surface to be joined and clamp with spring clamps spaced about 6″ to 12″ apart. Allow the cement to harden for several hours, then trim the edge flush with a straight router bit guided with a straightedge. A decorative edge may be routed if desired.

Corian can be substituted for the wood front build-up strip. This may be left square-cornered or shaped as shown.

15 | Projects with Corian

While Corian was developed as a building product primarily for kitchen and bath applications, this doesn't preclude using it as a medium for creative work. With the same tools and techniques used for ordinary woodworking and a supply of the material, you can make truly attractive decorative or functional pieces equaled only by real marble. The following projects are examples of the possibilities.

CLOCK OF CORIAN.   This modern version of the stately grandfather pendulum clock is a challenging project which will be well worth the effort. You'll get all the pieces required out of one ¾" × 30" × 96" panel with a bit to spare. The side-panel dropouts will provide precious scraps for other projects.

To keep the design clean, the slabs of Corian are assembled around two boxes made of ¾" plywood to permit driving bolts from the inside with no exposed heads. These bolts are turned into tapped holes in the Corian; used in conjunction with panel adhesive, they assure a solid assembly.

To drop out the side-panel openings, bore a hole 1½" in diameter at each corner. This hole size gives you the ¾" radius that is part of the design. It also lets you snug your saber-saw blade up tangent to the circle so the cut line will follow through without an offset.

Saw from hole to hole, using a clamped straightedge for a guide. You'll need patience for this task; using a 14-tooth-per-inch metal-cutting blade, the rate of cut will be about 1½" per minute.

After you've cut out the openings for the pendulum and weight chains, attach the Corian to the top plywood box, which serves as the movement enclosure. Bolt (from inside) into the top and bottom facing slabs, using ¼–20 × 1" FH stove bolts.

When repeating this step for the bottom box, you must work through the box, because space is tight. After you've bored through both plywood panels with a long bit of proper diameter for the lead holes, enlarge the

Clock of Corian is a challenging project that requires patience.

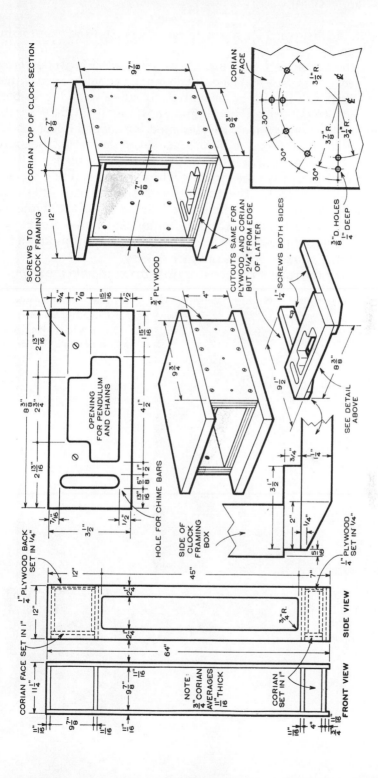

CORIAN TOP OF CLOCK SECTION

SCREWS TO CLOCK FRAMING

CORIAN FACE

$3\frac{1}{2}$ R.

$3\frac{7}{8}$ R.

$3\frac{1}{4}$ R.

30°

30°

30°

$9\frac{7}{8}$

$9\frac{7}{8}$

$9\frac{3}{4}$

$7\frac{9}{16}$

12"

$\frac{3}{4}$" PLYWOOD

CUTOUTS SAME FOR PLYWOOD AND CORIAN BUT $2\frac{1}{4}$" FROM EDGE OF LATTER

$1\frac{1}{4}$" SCREWS BOTH SIDES

$\frac{3}{8}$"D. HOLES $\frac{1}{4}$" DEEP

$9\frac{1}{2}$

$8\frac{3}{8}$

SEE DETAIL ABOVE

$3\frac{1}{4}$

$\frac{7}{8}$

$1\frac{15}{16}$

$\frac{1}{2}$

$\frac{3}{4}$"PLYWOOD

$2\frac{13}{16}$

$1\frac{15}{16}$

4"

$9\frac{3}{4}$

$8\frac{3}{8}$

$2\frac{3}{4}$

OPENING FOR PENDULUM AND CHAINS

$4\frac{1}{2}$

$2\frac{13}{16}$

$1\frac{3}{16}$ $\frac{5}{8}$ 1" $\frac{1}{2}$

$\frac{7}{16}$

$3\frac{1}{2}$

$\frac{1}{2}$

HOLE FOR CHIME BARS

SIDE OF CLOCK FRAMING BOX

$\frac{3}{4}$

$\frac{1}{4}$

$3\frac{1}{2}$

2"

$\frac{1}{4}$

$5\frac{1}{16}$

1"PLYWOOD SET IN $\frac{1}{4}$"

PLAN

$\frac{1}{4}$" PLYWOOD BACK SET IN $\frac{1}{4}$"

12"

45"

7"

$2\frac{1}{4}$

12"

$2\frac{1}{4}$

$\frac{3}{4}$"R.

SIDE VIEW

CORIAN FACE SET IN 1"

$11\frac{1}{4}$

64"

$9\frac{7}{8}$ $1\frac{11}{16}$

NOTE: $\frac{3}{4}$" CORIAN AVERAGES $\frac{11}{16}$" THICK

CORIAN SET IN 1"

FRONT VIEW

$1\frac{11}{16}$

$9\frac{7}{8}$

$1\frac{11}{16}$

$\frac{3}{4}$ $3\frac{1}{16}$

4"

115

holes through the first panel for screwdriver access. Tap and countersink, then drive bolts.

To attach the other slab, you just drive 1½″ #8 FH wood screws through its face; this surface will face the floor and cannot be seen. Attach the upright side panels to both boxes with panel adhesive and stove bolts.

An eight-day weight-driven pendulum movement, HCS-2W, is the mechanism used for this project. It's designed for a weight drop of 52″; the clock's opening is a little shy, so figure on a seven-day cycle. The source of supply for the mechanism is listed in the back of this book.

So that the shaft that drives the hands will be in dead center on the face, you make a special rack. It has two runners with tapered ends—so shaped to let you fit the assembly into the enclosure. The longest of the chime bars projects about 3″ below the clock support frame; the tapered ends let you tilt the assembly into the enclosure so that this long bar drops into a hole bored through the Corian for this purpose.

Wood screws on the runners, accessible from the rear, hold the assembly

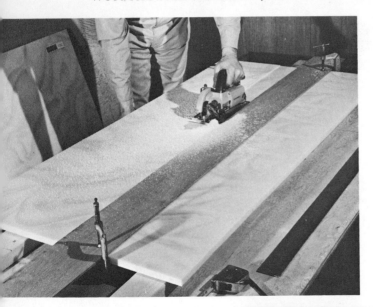

The slab is too heavy to handle on a table saw, so it is best cut to working size with a portable circular saw.

Large-diameter entry holes for saber saw form round corners of proper radius. Bell-type hole saw or spade bit can be used.

in place, but don't drive these until the exact forward location is determined by putting the movement up to the back surface of the clockface slab.

Since extra-long driving shafts are nonstandard, you'll probably have to reduce the thickness of this slab down to ½″ (you could substitute a face of ¼″-thick Corian, but it would mean an extra purchase). The recess can be made with a router or on the drill press using a mortising router bit. Drive four ¾″ bolts through the vertical members of the clock framing and into tapped sockets in the back of the face. These sockets must be quite shallow (not over ⅜″ deep).

The clockface markers are short lengths of ⅜″ brass rod set in sockets so as to project about ¼″. Chuck each of these plugs into a drill and work them with abrasive paper to obtain a satin finish.

To function properly, a pendulum clock must be perfectly level, so make your final check not in your workshop but at the location where the clock is to be displayed.

For tangent cut, snug blade against side of hole and clamp straightedge along base of saber saw.

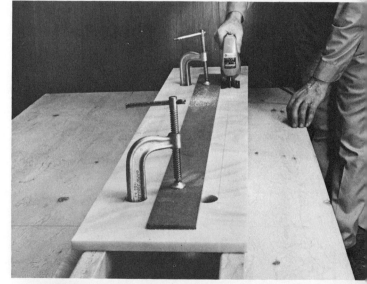

Sand all edges and break all sharp corners. Using very fine abrasive and a finish sander for final pass, you can achieve a polish to match that of the face.

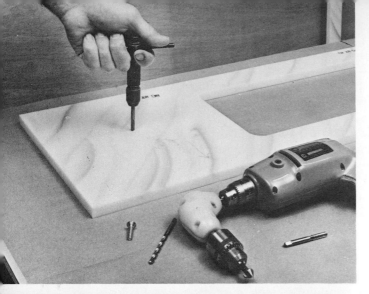

Threading shallow holes is tricky, to avoid stripping. Bore to depth of ⅝" and thread with bottoming tap for countersunk screws.

Right-angle drill accessory is needed for tight spot in upper box. Wood block limits depth of hole and keeps bit perpendicular.

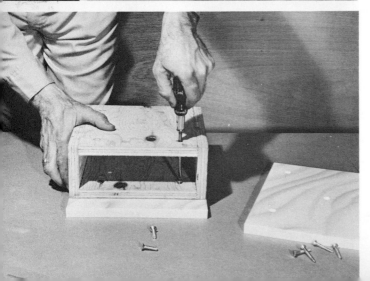

Spacing of lower block is even tighter. Drill and drive through plywood bottom to attach upper slab. Then add lower slab.

The upper and lower components ready for final assembly.

Panel adhesive and machine screws hold the parts together. An offset screwdriver is necessary for the lower box.

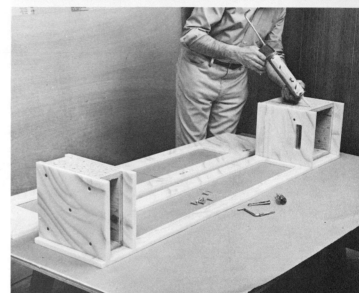

With chime bar removed, clock shelf looks like this. Bar, lower right, screws in from top.

A drill press or router can be used to recess the back of the clockface panel.

Bolts through clock frame secure the face panel.

Cement the brass number plugs into shallow sockets with a dab of adhesive. Two plugs are used at four points for easier reading of time.

SUPERGRAPHIC TABLETOP. This disk of Corian serves two functions. Hung on a wall, it creates a bold decorative accent. Lifted off the wall, it fits neatly on a plywood cube table to provide a more spacious top when needed. The wall mounting bracket is permanently attached to the wall.

The plan calls for ¾"-thick Corian, but if you don't mind a lamination joint around the edges, you can use less costly ¼" sheet to face ½" plywood, joining the two with contact cement.

Splitting the top in two not only creates a striking design, it lets you get a larger diameter than is otherwise possible with a 30"-wide Corian sheet. The two halves which make up the top represent a 36"-diameter circle with a 1" gap in between. In order to obtain two true half circles, the pivot point of the saber saw circle guide is offset ½" beyond the edge of the panel. This is done by clamping a block of wood alongside the edge.

A large-diameter circle guide can be homemade with a piece of mild steel bar stock. Hammer one end over to form an L, then drill a pivot hole in alignment with the front of the blade teeth. Mount the bar in the guide channel of the saw. Cut the two half disks using a 14-tooth-per-inch metal-cutting blade.

Use a router with a corner-rounding cutter to form a small radius on the edges of both disks. Place the finished disks face down on a flat surface, then position the wood cleats. Drill pilot holes through the cleats and partly into the Corian. Set the cleats aside and thread the holes in the Corian with a ¼–20 tap. Before assembly, drill the ⅜" holes in the upper

Corian tabletop also serves as decorative wall accent.

The Corian top in place on its plywood cube base.

PLAN

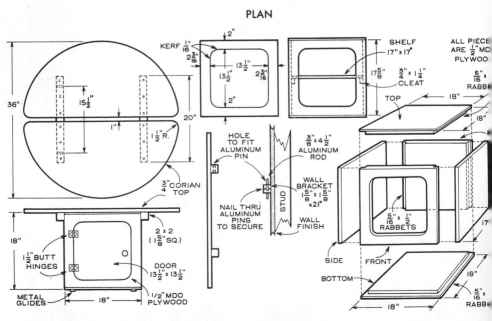

cleat (at right angles to, and spaced between, the bolt holes) to take the wall bracket pins.

To ensure alignment, have the wall bracket already assembled. This bracket should match the dimensions of the tabletop cleats. Use aluminum or solid-brass rod for the pins. Lock the pins in place with a nail driven through a pre-drilled hole in each rod.

Apply a wavy bead of panel adhesive to the back of the Corian before repositioning the cleats and bolting them fast. Mount the bracket at the desired height on your wall, bridging two studs if possible. Lag bolts (or husky toggle bolts, if you must anchor to a hollow wall) are suggested, because the disk is heavy.

The cube is constructed with ½" MDO (medium density overlaid) plywood, surfaced two sides. This is suggested because its coated surface is ideal for painting, but ordinary plywood may be used instead. Use any color that picks up an accent in your room's furnishings. Paint the tabletop cleats to match.

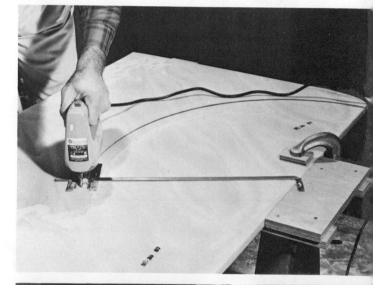

The pivot point of the circle guide is positioned ½" beyond the edge of the sheet of Corian in order to obtain a section that is less than a half circle.

All edges are eased with a self-piloted corner-rounding cutter. Finish off by sanding.

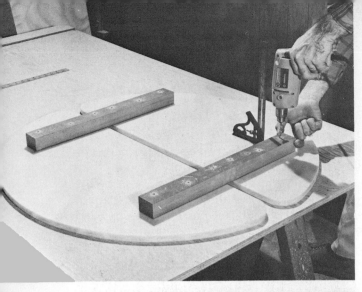

Position cleats with double-faced tape while drilling bolt holes through and partly into Corian. Counterbore for heads.

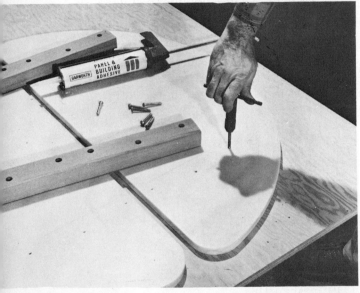

Remove the cleats, tap threads for the bolts.

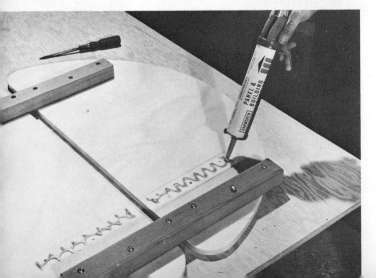

Apply bead of paneling adhesive to cleat position, keeping Corian halves 1" apart. Seat cleat in adhesive, drive bolts.

16 | Decorative Laminates

Plastic laminate is probably one of the most widely utilized materials for a variety of home-remodeling and new-construction applications. Attractiveness, durability, and ease of maintenance are the factors which account for its ever-increasing popularity as an important surfacing material ever since its introduction in the mid-1920s.

Laminate sheet was originally used mainly by industry and professional fabricators, because its application to a surface entailed relatively difficult and time-consuming gluing procedures. But the development of contact cement and its effectiveness as a bonding agent for the material has significantly simplified the process. Laminate has since gained wide appeal as a do-it-yourself material.

Working with laminate is not difficult and doesn't require any special skills. Once you learn the basics, you will have acquired the know-how to handle any job from the simple to the complex. The techniques used to surface a simple cube table, for example, will also work on a project such as surfacing a kitchen countertop, a cabinet, or whatever.

A cube table project might well illustrate the ease of working with laminate. Assuming you want such a table, you would start by constructing a square box with simple exposed butt joints using ordinary plywood. Since it will be covered, no fussy finish sanding will be necessary. Nor will you have to agonize over how to obtain a perfect finish, which frequently stumps many craftsmen on straight woodworking projects.

Using basically the same skills required to construct the box itself, you proceed to cut and apply to each surface squares of laminate of your choice; perhaps a brilliant color or an exotic woodgrain or marble pattern.

Suddenly the plain box is converted into a beautifully finished, attractive piece of furniture, worthy of occupying a place of prominence in any room of the house. That's about the gist of it.

You'll discover that transforming the ordinary into a thing of beauty can be quite satisfying, and economical, too. There is a real potential for saving

This elegant vanity top is surfaced with marble-patterned laminate; the cabinet is surfaced in rich woodgrain.

Formica

Wilsonart

An ordinary square box surfaced with laminate becomes a fine piece of furniture.

Laminate surfacing is advantageous for youth furniture, which must withstand abuse.

on high labor costs by doing your own remodeling work with plastic laminate. Of course, you'll also save money by making your own furnishings or accessories instead of buying high-priced ready-mades.

Technically the material is described as high-pressure melamine-phenolic plastic laminate. In simple terms, it is made with a number of layers of kraft paper, a pattern sheet, and a protective top sheet, all impregnated with a variety of resins. The multilayered sandwich is subjected to heat and high pressure in a huge hydraulic press. The end result is a tough, dense, semirigid sheet which is highly resistant to water, abrasion, and staining by most household chemicals and alcohol.

This home-shop project was constructed with relatively low-cost fir plywood and surfaced with laminate. A store-bought piece of comparable quality would be quite costly.

SURFACES AND GRADES.   Plastic laminate sheet is available in a wide range of solid colors, decorative patterns, and simulated woodgrains, quarry materials, leathers, and many others. Some of the simulations have been developed to such a remarkable likeness in appearance and feel that they are quite often mistaken for the real thing.

There are a number of manufacturers producing laminate, but the brand names you'll most frequently encounter at local building-supply centers and lumberyards are Formica and Wilsonart. Their product lines are extensive, so you'll have no difficulty in obtaining a decorative surface to satisfy practically any need.

Laminates are available in several grades, including standard, vertical, backing, and post-forming. Surface finishes include gloss, satin, and furniture in addition to the textured surfaces.

The standard grade, $\frac{1}{16}''$ in thickness, is the choice for top (horizontal) surface applications which are subject to hard use, such as countertops, vanities, bars, tables, desks, and the like.

The vertical grade is $\frac{1}{32}''$ thick. It is used for cabinet and furniture sides, doors, light-duty shelving, window treatments, and walls. Rather flexible, it can be bent to a smaller radius than the standard grade. It is also less costly.

A small sampling of the numerous patterns, colors, and surfaces of plastic laminate.

Vertical-grade laminate is flexible and can readily be formed into small-radius curves.

Post-formed laminate countertops are available for do-it-yourself installations.

Wilsonart

Backing-grade sheet is plain, without a decorative face. Available in $\frac{1}{16}$" and $\frac{1}{32}$" thicknesses, it is used on the back of large, unsupported core material which would otherwise tend to warp as a result of unbalanced construction. For example, a laminate-surfaced tabletop supported all around by an apron would require no backing, but a hinged free-hanging drop leaf on this table definitely would require backing.

The post-forming grade is a special-purpose material which can be formed into a small radius. It is used by professional fabricators for various wrap-around applications such as one-piece seamless countertops which include a backsplash and rolled front edge. Special equipment is used to heat and form the sheet to the contours of a prefabricated substrate.

Post-forming sheet is of no practical value for home workshop use, but post-formed countertop modules which you can install yourself are available from retail dealers.

SHEET SIZES. Widths are usually available in 24", 30", 36", 48", and 60". Lengths run 60", 72", 84", 96", 120", and 144". Most sheets come slightly over the stated sizes to conveniently permit finish trimming to standard-size core materials. Another advantage of the slight oversize is that it allows for saw-kerf waste when subdividing into a smaller standard size—for example, cutting two 18" widths from a 36"-wide sheet. This suggests a consideration when designing projects: Whenever possible, try to keep dimensions of the work compatible to stock sizes or equal subdivisions, in the interest of economy. For example, much waste would result in designing a tabletop measuring 31" × 60" instead of 30" × 60". The latter is a stock size, the other is not.

17 | Working with Laminates

Though it is quite hard, laminate is thin and brittle and does not possess great strength and high impact resistance until it is bonded to a solid and dimensionally stable core.

CORE MATERIALS. Laminate can be applied to solid lumber, plywood, particleboard, and hardboard and also over old or worn laminate. Plywood and particleboard are recommended for new work. Whatever the surface to be covered, it must be flat, smooth, clean, and dry.

All voids in the core material must be filled with wood-filling compound and sanded flush. It is particularly important to fill even the smallest voids along the edges of the core, including the holes made by setting nail heads. The router cutter pilot end will follow any void during the trimming operation, resulting in an indent in the laminate edge.

Surface projections and hardened glue lumps at joints should be sanded flat to permit the laminate to make good contact. A belt or finishing sander will prove useful for smoothing or leveling large surfaces, but it must be used with care to avoid causing depressions and rounded edges. Small areas are handled by hand with abrasive paper backed with a block of wood.

Old laminate which is to be resurfaced with new should be thoroughly sanded to give it "tooth" for proper adhesive bond. Painted and clear-finished surfaces usually don't stand up well under the adhesive used to bond the laminate and therefore should be sanded down to the bare wood or other substrate.

TOOLS. There are several basic steps involved in surfacing with laminate, including cutting, applying adhesive, bonding, and trimming. The tools required to perform these operations are relatively few. As is true with many fabrication procedures, there are several tools which may be

A sound, flat surface is a prerequisite for a good laminate application. Voids should be filled, projections sanded flat, but finish quality sanding is not required.

used to achieve the same end result. Therefore you have a choice of options depending upon the size of the job and/or the speed with which you wish to accomplish the task. Of course the availability of a particular tool is also a factor.

Actually, you could do practically any job using only a few hand tools. These would include: rule, laminate scriber, fine-tooth handsaw, smooth-cut file, brush, hammer, and wood block.

For speedier cutting with less effort you could use any one of a choice of power saws, including: table saw, band saw, portable circular saw, and saber saw. Circular-type saws should be equipped with small-tooth plywood or carbide-tipped blades; the others, preferably with metal-cutting blades.

A router with straight and bevel cutters is the ideal tool for trimming edges. It may also be used for cutting. A special power laminate trimmer, similar to the router in construction and operation, is also available. It does both straight and bevel trimming with one adjustable cutter. Lacking these, the file is used for trimming.

Additional accessory tools might include a roller, a hair dryer or flame-less heat gun, and a power sander.

CUTTING. Standard procedure is to cut laminate sheet about ½" wider and longer than the size of the surface to which it is to be applied. This allows an overhang of about ¼" on all edges to facilitate alignment during bonding. The overhang also permits obtaining precise butt joints through flush trimming methods.

Trimming to size is accomplished after bonding. If hand trimming with a file is anticipated, it is advisable to allow only about ⅛" overhang in order to minimize the handwork. There is one exception to the overhang allowance rule: When the laminate is to be applied to an enclosed area it is cut to exact size beforehand.

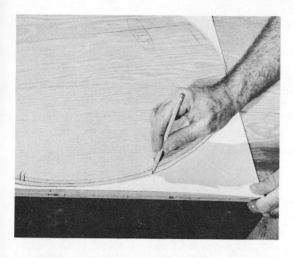

Laminate is cut slightly larger than the core material to which it is to be bonded, to allow for trimming.

Scribing.   Standard-grade (1/16″) laminate can be cut by scribing and breaking if suitable sawing equipment is not available. This method is particularly advantageous when working with vertical-grade (1/32″) sheet because it is so quick and easy.

Place the sheet on a firm, flat work surface, face side up, and use a metal straightedge to guide the scribing tool. This is the same tool used for scribing acrylics. Since the surface is rather slippery, the guide should be clamped in place to prevent it from shifting. If this is not feasible, a strip of masking tape applied to the bottom surface of the guide will provide some traction.

On the heavier material, make several passes to cut about halfway through. Then, while pressing on the guide strip, lift up on the free side to snap it off. The thinner sheet will require fewer passes with the tool. It may, in fact, be cut clear through with the scriber or a sharp utility knife.

Vertical-grade (1/32″) laminate can easily be cut with a sharp knife.

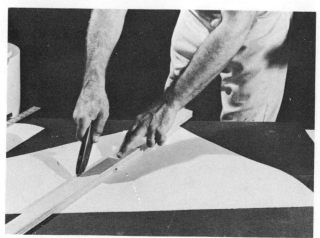

Sawing.   A 12- to 15-point crosscut handsaw can be used to cut laminate. Hold the saw at a very low angle, almost horizontal, and apply cutting pressure only on the forward stroke. The decorative side should be up.

When using a saber saw, which cuts on the upstroke, the decorative side is faced down in order to confine any chipping that may occur to the back of the sheet. Support the sheet along both sides of the cutting line over a pair of boards.

The portable circular saw also cuts on the upturn of the blade, so the decorative side should face down. The sheet can be supported along both sides of the cutting line as with the saber saw.

On the table saw the decorative side faces up. This applies also for the band saw and jigsaw. Long sheets which overhang the saw table should be supported at the back or side, as required. A problem usually encountered on the table saw is that the edge of the thin sheet slides into the space below the rip fence. The remedy is simple: Clamp a board to the fence with the bottom edge resting firmly on the table.

The table saw is invaluable for cutting laminate to exact finish size (no overhang). Always make a test on scrap to determine whether the cut edge will be sufficiently smooth for the purpose. If not, the piece should be cut slightly oversize to allow for sanding to size. Take the same precautions when making exact-size cuts with either of the hand power saws.

To cut laminate with a router, use a narrow-diameter (⅛″) straight cutter and a clamped straight guide. The same cutter may be used to make a perfectly matched cut for pieces which are to be surface-butted. The procedure is simple: Overlap the two sheets about 1 inch, making certain that the long edges are in alignment. Clamp both sheets to bottom supports spaced apart slightly to clear the cutter. Guide the router base against a clamped guide and make one pass to cut both sheets simultaneously.

ADHESIVE.   Laminate can be bonded to the core material with various types of adhesives. However, contact cement is preferred. It holds exceptionally well and does not require sustained pressure or long setting time. The work can be handled and further tooled immediately after contact of the parts.

Contact cements come in both flammable and nonflammable varieties. While these are equally good, the nonflammable latex-based kind is favored for use in the home because of the safety aspect and easy tool cleanup with water. If you choose to work with the flammable cement be certain to observe the usual safety precautions: no open flames, no sparking motors or door bells, and adequate ventilation.

The cement may be applied with paintbrush, serrated spreader, or roller. Most cements work best at temperatures above 65° F. and with low humidity.

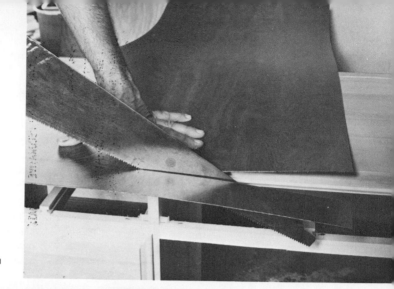

A crosscut saw is held at a low angle to cut laminate.

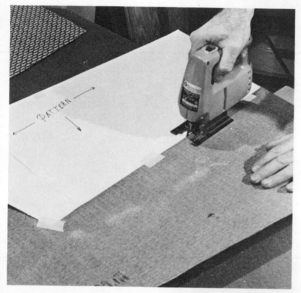

Face the decorative side down when cutting laminate with a saber saw. Here a pattern is used for cutting an irregular shape to exact size.

The jigsaw is especially useful for making intricate cutouts. Chipping problems are eliminated with the use of a fine-tooth blade.

Applying adhesive with a brush. Excessive brushing should be avoided, as it thins out the coating, resulting in a poor bond.

A notched spreader works faster than a brush but is not suitable for small areas such as edges.

A paint roller does the fastest spreading job, but the project should be large enough to justify the tool clean-up chore.

After cutting, laminate sheet usually has some partially loosened chips of material along the edges of the back. It is very important to scrape them off before applying cement, because any that become dislodged and embedded in the cement film will prevent good contact between the joining surfaces.

Contact cement differs from conventional adhesives in that after spreading, the adhesive must be allowed to air-dry before a satisfactory bond can be made. This drying period will vary, depending upon temperature and humidity, but usually will range between 15 and 30 minutes.

Application.   Spread or brush a uniform coat of adhesive on both surfaces, covering the entire bond area. Laminate sheet requires only one coat, but porous materials sometimes require two. With this in mind, always apply the adhesive to the core first. If it soaks up the adhesive, hold off the application on the laminate until the first coat on the core has dried sufficiently to receive the second coat. In this way the first coat on the laminate and the second coat on the core can have the same time to dry.

A good bond cannot be made unless the adhesive is sufficiently dry. Bonding readiness is determined by sight and touch. When first applied, the adhesive is cloudy. It will become glossy and clear when dry. For a positive final check, touch a piece of kraft (brown wrapping) paper to the surface. If the paper does not stick, the time is right. The working time for making the bond is usually one hour. Recoating will be necessary if the bond is not made within this time. Any dull spots on the original application indicate the need for a second coat.

Bonding.   When the adhesive-coated surfaces are brought into contact the bond will be immediate and permanent. The laminate cannot be shifted for repositioning once it touches down; therefore, alignment must be exact. The task is not especially difficult, since the oversize laminate affords some leeway in positioning. Using either the slip-sheet or slip-stick method, proper alignment and bonding will be assured.

Slip-sheet.   Cut two pieces of kraft paper, each piece slightly larger than half the size of the surface to be covered. Place the two sheets of paper on the core material, positioned to cover the entire area, overlapping a few inches at the center and overhanging the edges slightly. Place the laminate over the paper, then position it so it overhangs all the edges of the core.

Without pressing too hard, hold the laminate at one end so it doesn't shift, then gently slip out the paper at the opposite end. When initial contact is made, the laminate will no longer be able to shift. Allow contact to be made. Next, lift the laminate at the free end slightly upward and withdraw the second sheet of paper. While still holding the laminate away from the core, apply finger pressure. Begin at the contacted end and work toward the free end, gradually lowering the laminate to the core.

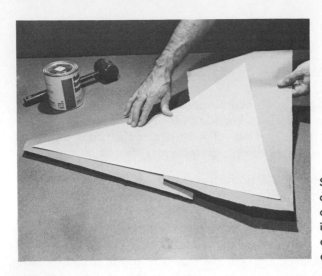

Slip-sheet method for aligning the laminate to the core. The laminate bonds immediately when the cement-coated surfaces make contact.

It should be noted that since the contacting surfaces grip quite aggressively with magnetic-like attraction, you must take care to avoid pressing down along the center area until the second sheet has been withdrawn. Otherwise the leading edge of the paper may become pinched in place, making removal quite difficult.

Slip-stick. This alternate method utilizes a series of sticks of wood instead of paper to keep the adhesive-coated surfaces out of contact while registration is made.

Use clean sticks which are free of sawdust or splinters and space them about 10″ or 12″ apart on the core. Stick thickness can range from about ¼″ to ½″. The use of thinner sticks is not advisable, especially when working with ¹⁄₃₂″ laminate, because the thin laminate may dip and make unintentional contact. On the other hand, sticks which are too thick will make visual edge alignment difficult.

When the laminate sheet is in alignment, pull out the sticks, one at a time, starting at an end. Apply hand pressure to the laminate progressively as the sticks are removed.

Final pressure. Clamp pressure is not required with contact cement, but momentary firm pressure is, in order to ensure complete intimate contact.

Pressure can be applied with a hammer and wood block or with a small roller. In either case, start at the center and work out toward the edges. When using the hammer, strike the block sharply and work systematically to make certain the entire surface is covered. If the laminate is one with a textured surface, use a felt padding on the block to distribute the pressure more evenly.

The roller also should be traveled over the entire surface with firm pressure. There is one important precaution to observe when using the roller: You must never run it off an overhanging edge. If you do, it will invariably result in breaking the unsupported portion of the laminate. Though the overhang will be trimmed off, such a break could reach slightly into the good area. Always move a roller parallel to an edge.

TRIMMING.   Trimming is carried out in two stages: preliminary-flush and bevel-finish trimming.

When two pieces of laminate are to be butted to form an outside corner, the overhang of the first piece bonded to the core must be trimmed flush to the work edge so that a good butt joint can be made when the second piece is applied. The overhang of the second piece also must be trimmed —not flush, however, but to a bevel. The bevel is comfortable to the touch and is not likely to chip and fray as would a sharp square corner. The trimming operation can be accomplished with a file or with a router.

Filing.   Use a flat smooth mill file. To trim the overhang flush to a core edge, hold the file on a plane with the core edge. Do not rock the file. Apply pressure only on the forward stroke and lift the file away on the return stroke to prevent chipping of the finish surface. Continue filing until the laminate edge is perfectly flush to the core.

When filing to finish an edge to a bevel, hold the file to produce an angle of about 25°. If any ripples develop, draw the file laterally along the edge.

Routing.   Flush and bevel trimming is most quickly and effectively accomplished with a router equipped with the appropriate cutter. Ordinary steel cutters dull rapidly and thus should be avoided. Special flush and

Use a roller or hammer and wood block to apply final pressure for good contact. Don't allow roller to ride over end overhangs or laminate may crack.

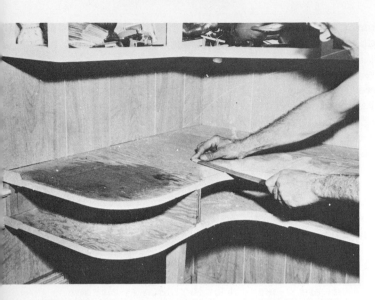

Using a file to flush-trim an edge. The file must be held perfectly flat to avoid rounding or beveling the edge.

bevel carbide cutters are recommended. They are ball-bearing self-piloted. The pilot rides against the edge of the work to guide the cut automatically.

The flush trimmer has a long cutting edge, which permits it to be alternately used for trimming thick wood edges. When making a flush cut, adjust the cutter so it projects just barely beyond the thickness of the laminate. The adjustment is not critical but it is best to avoid a deep projection, particularly when the router base is riding on a narrow work edge. The reason is that if the router is erratically tipped backward the blade could dig in and damage the work.

A router with carbide cutter makes quick work of trimming laminate overhang.

The projection adjustment of the bevel cutter is critical, because a cut which is too deep will expose the core. It is good practice to make a test cut on scrap work first. Otherwise, make the adjustment in small increments, and make the first cut on the least conspicuous part of the job and check it for accuracy before proceeding.

For a final finish, sand all beveled joints lightly with 400 grit paper on a block to smooth and soften the corners of the bevel.

EDGE TREATMENT.   Several kinds of edge treatment are possible for laminate fabrications, including self-edge, wood edge, and metal edge. Self-edge means using the same material for the edge as is used for surfacing—laminate. This is the most popular method of treating an edge.

The question of which surface to apply first must be considered when a self-edge is to be applied. This will depend upon the particular application. In general, the joint line should appear on the surface which is least conspicious and less subject to abuse. On a countertop or tabletop, the edge is applied before the top panel. The same applies for a backsplash and cabinet door. If a backsplash has an exposed end, the end strip goes on before the top edge. The front is last. Cabinet front edges are usually applied last. The same is true with decorative open shelving, in which the order would be: top, bottom, ends, front.

Countertops and tabletops are more attractive when the thickness is built up by adding a strip of wood to the bottom edges. A 1½" thickness is usually suitable for countertops, whereas on tables the thickness may range from 1" to 2" or more, depending upon general proportions.

When an edge has a small-radius curve it will be necessary to heat the laminate strip in order to give it the added flexibility required to make the bend without breaking. A hair dryer, heat gun, or heat lamp may be used

A laminate trimmer uses one cutter for both flush and bevel trimming. It is basically a router with a special base which has a built-in guide.

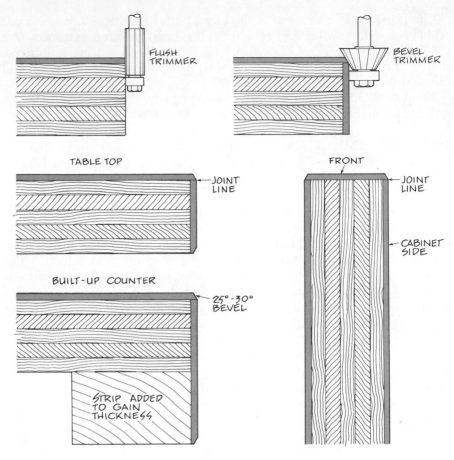

FLUSH TRIMMER

BEVEL TRIMMER

TABLE TOP

JOINT LINE

FRONT

JOINT LINE

CABINET SIDE

BUILT-UP COUNTER

25°-30° BEVEL

STRIP ADDED TO GAIN THICKNESS

EDGE TREATMENTS

to heat the piece. The strip is applied to the straight portion of the edge first, then heat is applied to the strip in the area of the bend immediately before making the turn. Two coats of adhesive should be applied to the core.

A wood edge, either plain or shaped, is sometimes called for in a design. This is usually added on after the laminate has been applied to the adjoining surface. Preferably, the wood should be completely shaped in advance so no further machining will be necessary.

Metal edges are available in snap-on and T drive-in styles. The T type requires a saw kerf to be cut into the edge of the workpiece. Though they are often used in commercial applications, metal edgings are not especially popular for use in the home.

18 | Projects with Laminates

Following are some ideas for putting laminates to use in simple fabrications. Once you acquire a little experience in working with the material you'll have the confidence to go on to bigger projects.

PLANTER. This two-shelf planter is easy to surface, provided you follow the laminate application sequence carefully.

Cut the parts from ¾" plywood stock. Drill pilot holes for 1½" #8 FH wood screws as indicated, making sure to countersink for the heads.

Apply laminate to the faces of the shelf supports, to the long edges of the shelves, and to the edges of the side members. When the laminate is bonded, trim the overhangs.

Attach the shelf supports to the shelves, then proceed to apply the laminate to the top surfaces of the shelves. Also apply the laminate to the insides of the end members. Trim all these overhangs to a slight bevel.

Re-bore through the pilot holes in the end members to continue the

Wilsonart

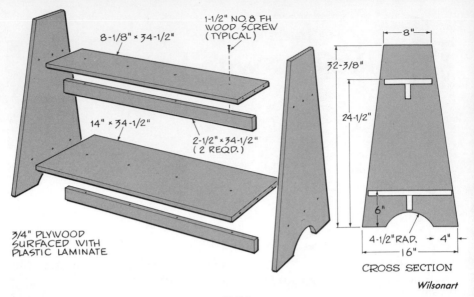

1-1/2" NO. 8 FH
WOOD SCREW
(TYPICAL)

8-1/8" × 34-1/2"

14" × 34-1/2"

2-1/2" × 34-1/2"
(2 REQD.)

3/4" PLYWOOD
SURFACED WITH
PLASTIC LAMINATE

8"

32-3/8"

24-1/2"

6"

4-1/2" RAD.   4"

16"

CROSS SECTION

Wilsonart

PLAN

holes in the laminate for the screws. Use a backup block to prevent chipping the laminate. Screw the end members to the shelves.

Apply the laminate to the outside of the end members, trim the overhang to a bevel, and finish off by sanding the corners lightly.

BOOKCASE. This unit is made of ¾" plywood and surfaced in much the same manner as the planter but with these minor differences: the shelves receive laminate only on one edge; and the laminate is applied to the outside of the shelf supports after they have been screwed to the shelves.

Wilsonart

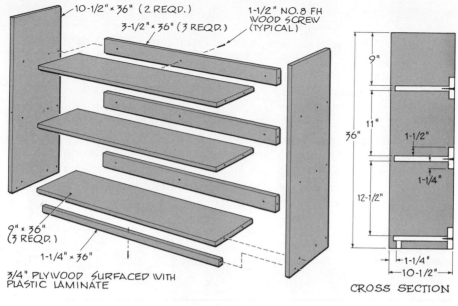

10-1/2" × 36" (2 REQD.)

3-1/2" × 36" (3 REQD.)

1-1/2" NO. 8 FH WOOD SCREW (TYPICAL)

9"

11"

36"

1-1/2"

1-1/4"

12-1/2"

9" × 36" (3 REQD.)

1-1/4" × 36"

3/4" PLYWOOD SURFACED WITH PLASTIC LAMINATE

1-1/4"

10-1/2"

CROSS SECTION

PLAN

SELF-EDGED COUNTERTOP.

The usual procedure in making a self-edged top, whether it be a counter or table, is to start by gaining edge thickness. Do this by gluing a strip of wood of the desired thickness along the bottom edge of the core. Use nails of the proper length so they don't protrude through the top surface.

Next, apply strips of laminate to the ends. Trim off the overhang flush to the core, then add the front strip and trim flush. At the same time, follow a similar procedure with the backsplash: Apply strips to the ends, then the top edge. The bottom edge of the backsplash does not receive laminate.

When all edge strips have been trimmed flush, apply contact cement to

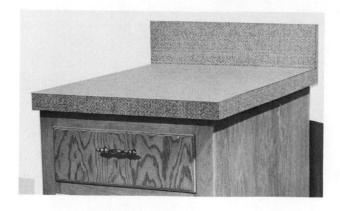

the laminate and core surfaces, both the top and backsplash. Allow the cement to set, align the laminate, bring it into contact with the core, and apply pressure with a hammer and block or with a roller.

Trim the edges flush, then rout or file a bevel and finish off with a light sanding of the bevel corners.

The backsplash is secured with screws inserted through the bottom of the core. Clamp the splash in place while drilling pilot holes for the screws. Apply a continuous bead of silicone sealant to the joint before driving the screws. Excess sealant which gets on the surface can be scraped off with a scrap of laminate. A metal scraping tool should be avoided because nicks in the edge could scratch the laminate.

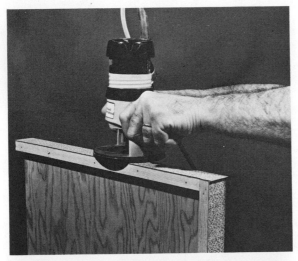

Apply laminate to edges first, then trim flush to core.

Coat the broad surfaces of the piece with adhesive.

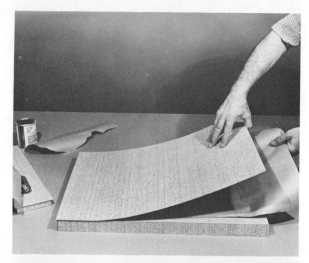

Align the laminate with overhang all around.

Trim off the excess flush to the edge. Follow with a bevel cutter.

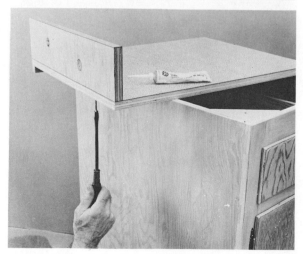

Apply sealant to joint, then screw in the backsplash.

A "slate"-topped table at a fraction of the cost and weight of the real thing— and better-wearing.

LAMINATE TABLETOP INSERTS. Tabletops can be made more interesting and better-wearing with laminate inserts. Two such treatments are illustrated. The top on the contemporary table features an insert of simulated slate. The other is topped with a richly grained leatherlike laminate (Wilsonart Latigo Leather). The "leather" is further enhanced with an elaborately detailed border accomplished by applying decorative decals.

The best way to make such a top is to apply the laminate to a separate core, which is then dropped into a framed construction. This results in a flush surface and assures a neat installation. Another advantage is that the adjoining wood surface can be freely and properly finish-coated before final assembly.

The tabletop should be designed with an open frame with a rabbet deep enough to receive the core and laminate thickness combined. Cut the core to size for a good fit into the recess before applying the laminate to the core. Apply the laminate slightly oversize, trim the edges flush, then ease the sharp corners by sanding with a block.

Applying a decal border is easy. Portions of ordinary water-applied

This "leather" top could fool the experts, and the embellishment looks like tooled gold leaf.

A rabbeted-frame construction is best, but a built-up edge can also be used. Dimension the core for a good fit.

decals are used to make the decorative border illustrated. The decals won't adhere properly to a textured laminate surface unless a special step is taken. The laminate is pre-coated with a liquid decoupage finish such as Aqua-Podge, which is available at handicraft and hobby shops. The coating is applied with a brush and allowed to dry.

The decal designs are dipped into warm water for about ten seconds, then placed face up on a damp towel. When the decal releases easily it is slid off the backing paper and into position on the laminate. A piece of unruled writing paper is placed over the decal, then pressed firmly with a small rubber roller. When the decals have dried, another coat of the finish is applied over the entire surface of the laminate.

Apply laminate to the core, then trim flush. Do not bevel the edges—ease them with light sanding.

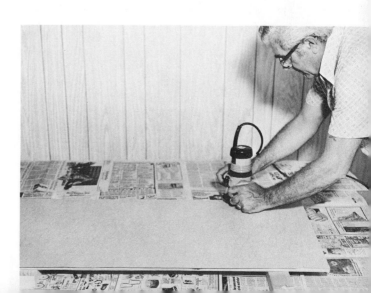

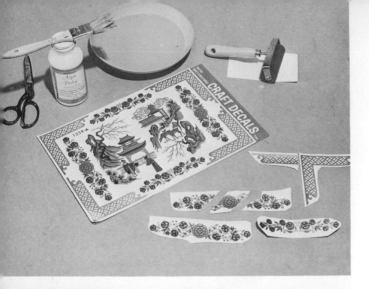

Apply a coat of decoupage finish to the laminate surface. Cut the decal sheet into strips as required.

Soak decals in water, then slide them into place. Apply pressure with a rubber roller over a sheet of paper.

The completed panel is glued into place.

A typical L-shaped post-formed countertop. It can be installed in several hours

POST-FORMED COUNTERTOP INSTALLATION. Replacement of a worn countertop or the addition of a top to new construction can be accomplished with relative ease if you install a post-formed ready-made. Available at most lumberyards and kitchen-counter dealers, these units feature a seam-free continuous laminate surface bonded to industrial-grade particleboard. They are available in straight lengths, or they can be ordered with mitered corners to form an L shape to fit a corner. A typical L-shaped kitchen countertop installation is shown.

Since the length of the countertop you will require may not be exactly a modular length, you should order the next larger size. When calculating size, be sure to allow for end overhang, which is usually about ¾". An end-cap kit which allows you to finish the end of the top with a matching laminate should also be purchased, together with special fastening bolts used for joining separate countertop sections to form a corner.

Before removing the old top, be sure to turn off and then disconnect water and electrical or gas lines. If you are planning to reinstall the existing sink or range, take note of the dimensions and locations of these openings for later use.

Check the top of the cabinet with a level to determine if it is level both lengthwise and front to back. If not, nail in shims to correct.

Measure and mark the countertop for length cutoff. Place a strip of masking tape across the entire width of the countertop at this point to prevent chipping during sawing. Re-draw the cutting line over the masking tape, then use a sharp crosscut handsaw (10 or 12 teeth per inch) to make the cut. Begin at the top of the backsplash, cut slowly, and apply pressure only on the forward stroke.

When cutting the holes for the sink or range, mark the cutout line on the top of the countertop as indicated by the old cutouts. If a new sink or range is to be installed, use the template or dimensions usually provided by the manufacturer. Drill pilot holes in each corner within the cutout area, then follow the cutting line, using a saber saw.

Before attaching laminate end caps, the bottom and back of the core at the cut ends must be filled out with wood blocks to form a solid base for the caps. Use short nails and glue to fasten the blocks. Apply contact cement to both surfaces. Bond the caps with a slight projection above the countertop. Use a router or file to trim off the excess.

To assemble the miter corners, turn the units bottom side up. Apply clear silicone sealant to both edges, then insert the fastening connectors and tighten to close the joint. Before final tightening, check to make sure the sections are flush and in alignment.

Secure the countertop by using wood screws through the cross members of the cabinets. Be sure the screws are the correct length so they will not protrude into the laminate.

Reinstalling the existing sink or range will be a reversal of the removal process. Apply plumber's putty or caulking compound to the rim of the sink. This should be done on a new sink as well.

Top left: Accessory kit includes pre-cut caps for left and right ends and fastening bolts. *Top right:* Mark cutoff line on masking tape and start the cut at the top of the backsplash, using a sharp, fine-tooth crosscut saw. *Bottom left:* Drill holes for the sink cutout in the waste area, tangent to the line. *Bottom right:* Saber-saw cutout, making sure there are no obstructions below the top. *Courtesy Wilsonart.*

Top left: Fill out the end of core with wood before attaching end cap. Apply contact cement to both surfaces. *Top right:* Trim off the excess, then bevel, using a router or smooth file. *Center:* Apply sealant to the miter joint and take up firmly on the connecting bolts. *Bottom left:* Apply plumber's putty liberally to the sink rim. *Bottom right:* Drop in sink and take up on fastening hardware to complete the project. *Courtesy Wilsonart.*

Materials and Tool Sources

The materials and tools described in this book are nationally distributed and generally are readily available. If you have difficulty in locating a local source of supply, write to the manufacturers. The clock movement is a specialty mail-order item.

ACRYLICS, TOOLS, AND ACCESSORIES

Rohm and Haas Company
Plexiglas Marketing Services
Consumer Plastics
Independence Mall West
Philadelphia, PA 19105

CORIAN

Corian Building Products
E. I. du Pont de Nemours Company
Wilmington, DE 19898

LAMINATES

Formica
Formica Corporation
Wayne, NJ 07470

Wilsonart
Ralph Wilson Plastics Company
600 General Bruce Drive
Temple, TX 76501

ALUMINUM STORM SASH

Reynolds Metals Company
Consumer Products
Richmond, VA 23261

MOTO-TOOL

Dremel Manufacturing Company
4915 21st Street
Racine, WI 53406

CLOCK MOVEMENT

Armor Products
P.O. Box 290
Deer Park, NY 11729
(Catalog $1)

AQUA PODGE; CASTING MATERIALS

American Handicrafts Company
P.O. Box 791
Ft. Worth, TX 76101

Index